Kafka's Other Trial

Elias Canetti

KAFKA'S OTHER TRIAL ~

The Letters to Felice

Translated by Christopher Middleton

Schocken Books • New York

S

Library of Congress Cataloging in Publication Data

Canetti, Elias, 1905–
    Kafka's other trial; the letters to Felice.
    Translation of Der andere Prozess.
    Includes bibliographical references.
    1. Kafka, Franz, 1883–1924—Correspondence.
2. Bauer, Felice, 1887–1960—Correspondence.
I. Title.
PT2621.A26Z64813   833'.9'12 [B]   74-3048

ISBN 0–8052–3553–1
ISBN 0–8052–0705–8 (paperback)

So now they are in print, these letters, telling of five years of torment; and the first name of Kafka's fiancée—the only pointer to which was for a long time the discreet sign "F.," matching Kafka's "K.," so that for many years people had no idea what she was called and were kept wondering which of all possible names it might be, never guessing the right one, for to do so was quite impossible—this name now stands writ large on the cover of the book. The woman to whom these letters were addressed died in 1960. Five years before her death, she sold them to Kafka's publisher; however this may strike one, Kafka's "dearest business-woman" certainly was showing for one last time that efficiency of hers, which meant much to him and even evoked feelings of tenderness in him.

True, Kafka had been dead for forty-three years when these letters appeared. Even then, because one revered the man and his misfortune, one's first response was a feeling of awkwardness and embarrassment. I know people whose embarrassment increased, the more they read, who could not help feeling that they were intruding precisely where they should not.

I respect these people, but I am not one of them. I found these letters more gripping and absorbing than any literary work I have read for years past. They belong among those singular memoirs, autobiographies, collections of letters from which Kafka himself drew sustenance. He himself, with reverence his loftiest feature, had no qualms about reading, over and over again, the letters of Kleist, of Flaubert, and of Hebbel. In one of the most harassed moments of his life, he took his cue from the fact that Grillparzer, when he was finally able to take Kathi Fröhlich on his lap, felt altogether indifferent (405).* In the face of life's horror—luckily most people notice it only on occasion, but a few whom inner forces appoint to bear witness are always conscious of it—there is only one comfort: its alignment with the horror experienced by previous witnesses. One must accordingly be most grateful to Felice Bauer for keeping and preserving Kafka's letters, even if she did find it in her heart to sell them.

To call these letters a document would be saying too little, unless one were to apply the same title to the life-testimonies of Pascal, Kierkegaard, and Dostoevski. For my part, I can only say that these letters have penetrated me like an actual life, and that they are now so enigmatic and familiar to me that it seems they have been mental possessions of mine from the moment when I first began to accommodate human beings entirely in my mind, in order to arrive, time and again, at a fresh understanding of them.

* Figures in parentheses included in the text refer to Franz Kafka, *Letters to Felice* (New York: Schocken Books, 1973; London: Martin Secker & Warburg, 1974).

It was in Max Brod's family apartment, on August 13, 1912, late in the evening, that Kafka first met Felice Bauer. Many remarks that he made at the time about this meeting have been preserved. The first occurs in a letter to Max Brod, dated August 14. Kafka here refers to the manuscript of *Meditation,* which he had brought to Brod on the previous evening; together they were to make a final arrangement of the texts in it. "Yesterday, when we were arranging the pieces, I was under the girl's influence, it is just possible that something foolish, some (secretly) comic sequence may have resulted."[1] He asks Brod to see that all is well, and he thanks him. The next day, August 15, the following statement appears in his diary: "Thought much of—what embarrassment before writing down names—F.B."[2]

Then on August 20, a week after the meeting, he tries to describe his first impression objectively. He describes her appearance, and feels that he is becoming a little estranged from her by "coming too close to her, physically," in this description. He found it natural that she, a stranger, should be sitting in this company. He got on well with her at once. "As I was sitting down, I looked at her closely for the first time, by the time I was seated I already had an unshakable verdict."[3] The diary entry breaks off in the middle of the next sentence. All the weightier observations might otherwise have been set down; how much more might have been written becomes apparent only later.

He writes to her for the first time on September 20, and reminds her—five weeks have passed since their meeting—that he is the person at the Brods' apartment who handed to her, across the table, one by one, some photographs, "and who finally, with the very hand now striking the keys, held your hand, the one which confirmed a promise to accompany him next year to Palestine" (5).

The promptness of this promise, the certainty with which she made it, were what impressed him so strongly at first. He senses in this handshake an avowal, the word betrothal lying not far behind it, and quickness cannot but fascinate him, slow as he is at making decisions himself, for whom every goal he would like to approach removes itself in a thousand doubts, instead of coming closer. The goal of the promise, however, is Palestine; and at this stage in his life there could hardly have been a more auspicious word—it is the Promised Land.

The situation becomes still more significant when one considers what pictures he is handing across the table. They are photographs of a "Thalia" journey: [4] early in July, five or six weeks before, he had been with Max Brod in Weimar, where some remarkable events had befallen him in the Goethe House. Inside the Goethe House itself he had noticed the custodian's daughter, a beautiful girl. He had managed to converse with her, had been introduced to her parents, had photographed her in the garden and at the entrance to the house, was invited to return and so could visit the house freely, not only during official visiting hours. Also, he met her often, by chance, in the lanes of the little town, watched her anxiously in company with young men, arranged a rendezvous with her, which she did not keep, and soon came to realize that her preference was for students. The whole thing happened during a period of a few days; the encounter had gained in intensity by being part of the movement of travel, which makes everything happen at a quicker pace. Immediately after this, Kafka went alone, without Brod, to a sanatorium at Jungborn, in the Harz Mountains. There are wonderfully rich memoirs of those weeks, free from "Thalia" interests and pious respect for the dwellings of great poets. But he sent postcards to the beautiful girl in Weimar, and received answers. He copies out one of the answers verbatim in a letter to Brod, and adds the following remark—a hopeful one, considering his cast of mind: "For even if I do not displease her, yet she finds me utterly humdrum. But why then does she write, just as I want her to? Could it be that one can take a girl captive by writing?"[5]

So the encounter in the Goethe House gave him courage. Across the table he hands to Felice the pictures taken on that journey. The memory of his attempt to make contact, and of his doings at the time, which had led at least to the photographs he could now show, is transferred to the girl who sits facing him now: Felice.

Kafka also became acquainted with Ernst Rowohlt on this journey, which had begun in Leipzig, and Rowohlt had decided to publish his first book. The compiling of short prose pieces from his diaries, for the book *Meditation*, had been keeping Kafka very busy. He was hesitant; the pieces did not seem to him good enough. Brod pressed him and kept the pressure up; eventually the book took shape, and on the evening of August 13 Kafka brought the final selection with him, intending, as has already been remarked, to discuss the arrangement of them with Brod.

Thus he was equipped, on that evening, with everything that might bring him encouragement: the manuscript of his first book; the pictures of the "Thalia" journey, among them the pictures of the girl who had responded to him politely; and in his pocket an issue of the magazine *Palästina*.

Kafka felt at ease with the Brod family, in whose home the meeting occurred. He used to try, as he himself tells, to prolong the evenings spent with them, and when they wanted to get to bed he had to be driven away, albeit amicably. It was the family in which he took refuge from his own. Here literature was not taboo. Max Brod's parents were proud of their son and of the name he had already made as a writer, and they took his friends seriously.

It is also a time during which Kafka's notebook writings acquired a new scope and precision. The Jungborn diary entries—finest of all his travel diaries—testify to this. They are also the ones that relate most directly to his oeuvre proper, in this case to *Amerika*.

The richness of his memory for concrete detail is shown in the amazing sixth letter to Felice, dated October 27, in which he describes their meeting in the most precise terms. Seventy-five days have elapsed since the evening of August 13. Of the details of that evening, recorded in his memory, some have more importance than others. Some he notes almost, one might say, with truculence, to show her that he had missed no detail of her person, that nothing had escaped him. He shows how much he is a Flaubertian writer, from whom nothing is trivial as long as it is right. With a touch of pride he presents the whole picture, doing a twofold honor—to her, because she was worthy to be comprehended, at once, in every detail; but some honor he does also to himself, to his own all-seeing eye.

On the other hand he observes one or another detail because it has significance for him, because it conforms to important traits in his own nature, because it balances out some deficiency of his, or because it astonishes him and brings him, through wonderment, physically closer to her. These are the details to be discussed here, because it is these that shape his image of her during the next seven months. That image persists until he sees her again, and about half of their very ample correspondence consists of letters written during these seven months.

She paid very serious attention to the "Thalia" photographs and only looked up when an explanation was given, or when he handed her another picture; she neglected her food on account of the pictures, and when Max made a remark about this she said that there was nothing more abhorrent to her than people who were constantly eating. (Kafka's restraint in matters of eating will be discussed later on.) She told how, when small, she had often been beaten by her brothers and cousins and had been quite defenseless against such beatings. She ran her hand down her left arm, which, so she said, had been covered with bruises. Yet she did not look sorry for herself; and he could not imagine how anyone could have dared to strike her, even if in those days she had been only a little girl. He has in mind his own frailty during childhood, but, unlike him, she has not gone on feeling sorry for herself. He looks at her arm and marvels at its present strength—no trace of any earlier childhood weakness.

She remarked casually, while examining or reading something, that she had studied Hebrew. He marveled at this, but would have preferred her not to have mentioned it in such an exaggeratedly casual way; and so he was secretly delighted when, later on, she could not translate Tel Aviv. But then it also transpired that she was a Zionist, and this suited him very well.

She said that she enjoyed copying manuscripts and asked Max to send her some. Kafka was so amazed by this that he banged on the table.

She was on her way to a wedding in Budapest. Frau Brod mentioned a pretty batiste dress she had seen in Felice's hotel room. Then everyone stood up to go from the dining room into the music room. "When you got up it turned out that you were wearing Frau Brod's slippers, because your shoes had to be dried. The weather had been terrible all day. These slippers bothered you a bit, and while walking through the dark center room, you told me you were used to slippers with heels. Such slippers were new to me" (15). The older woman's slippers bothered her; her description of her own kind of slippers, at the end of their passage through the dark center room, brought him physically even more close to her than the contemplation of her arm, which had no bruises on it now.

Later, when everyone was leaving, something else occurred: "I could not get over the speed with which you finally scurried out of the room, and returned in your shoes" (16). Here the speed of the transformation impresses him. His kind of transformation is the opposite, almost always a singularly slow process, which he has to verify step by step before he can believe in it. He constructs his transformations with the thoroughness and precision of a mason building a house. There she was, standing before him suddenly, a woman in shoes, yet she had just scurried out of the room in slippers.

Previously he had mentioned, though only in passing, that he happened to have an issue of the magazine *Palästina* with him. The journey to Palestine was discussed and it was then that she offered to shake his hand, "or rather, thanks to an inspiration, I extracted it from you" (16). Brod's father and Kafka then accompanied her to her hotel. On the street he lapsed into one of his "semitrances" (16) and behaved clumsily. He also heard that she had left her umbrella in the train, and this trifling detail added a new dimension to his picture of her. She was to leave early the next morning: "That you had not yet packed, and still intended to read in bed, made me uneasy. During the previous night you had read until four in the morning" (17). Despite his concern about her early departure, this trait must have added to the familiarity he felt toward her: he himself wrote at night.

In general, one comes to see Felice as a definite personality, who responds to other people quickly and openly, and who will unhesitatingly pronounce an opinion on any subject.

The correspondence developed rapidly. with daily letters coming from Kafka and Felice soon replying at the same rate (only his letters are preserved). It has certain quite astonishing features: for an open-minded reader, the most noticeable is the amount of complaining, on Kafka's part, about his physical states. These complaints begin as early as the second letter, still somewhat veiled: "Oh, the moods I get into, Fräulein Bauer! A hail of nervousness pours down upon me continuously. What I want one minute I don't want the next. When I have reached the top of the stairs, I still don't know the state I shall be in when I enter the apartment. I have to pile up uncertainties within myself before they turn into a little certainty or a letter. . . . My memory is very bad . . . my halfheartedness . . . I remember that I once actually got out of bed to write down what I had thought out for you; but I promptly returned to bed, because—and this is my second failing—I reproached myself for the foolishness of my anxiety" (6-7).

One can see that what he is describing here is his indecisiveness, and with this his wooing begins. But soon everything is brought into relation to his physical states.

He begins the fifth letter with a reference to his inability to sleep, and he ends it with an account of interruptions in the office where he is writing. From now on, there is hardly a single letter without complaints. At first they are outweighed by interest in Felice. He asks a hundred ques-

11

tions, wants to know everything about her, wishes to be in a position to imagine exactly what goes on in the office where she works and in her home. But that sounds far too general —actually his questions are more concrete. He asks her to tell him when she arrives at her office, what she has had for breakfast, what sort of view she has from her office window, what sort of work she is doing. What are the names of her friends, men and women; who it is that is damaging her health with sweets—these are only the very first questions, countless others follow later. He wants her to be well and safe. He wants to know about the rooms she lives and works in, and no less about how she arranges her time. He will not let any contradiction pass, and he asks for immediate explanations. Of Felice he demands a precision equal to that with which he describes his own states of mind.

More will be said about these later; one must try to understand them, or one understands nothing. For the moment, let us keep in mind Kafka's deeper intent during the first period of this correspondence: he was establishing a connection, a channel of communication, between her efficiency and health and his own indecisiveness and weakness. Across the distance between Prague and Berlin he wishes to hold fast to her robustness. The weak words that he is permitted to address to her come back from her ten times stronger. He writes to her two or three times a day. He fights—contrary to his assertions about his weakness—tenaciously, even unyieldingly, for her answers. She is—in this one respect—more capricious than he; she does not have the same obsession. But he succeeds in imposing upon her his own obsession: soon enough, she too is writing him a letter a day, sometimes two.

The struggle to obtain this strength which her regular letters bring him does have meaning. It is no empty exchange of letters, no end in itself, no mere self-gratification: it helps his *writing*. Two nights after his first letter to her he writes "The Judgment," at one sitting, during a single night, in ten hours. One might say that with this story his self-assurance as a writer was established. He reads it to his friends, the story's authenticity is beyond doubt, and there-after he never repudiated it as he did so many other writings. During the following week he writes "The Stoker," and then inside the next two months five more chapters of *Amerika*, making six chapters altogether. During a two-week pause in the writing of the novel, he writes *The Metamorphosis*.

So it is a magnificent period, and not only from our later standpoint; few other periods in Kafka's life can be compared with it. To judge by the results—and how else should one judge a writer's life—Kafka's attitude during the first three months of correspondence with Felice was entirely the right one for him. He was feeling what he needed to feel: security somewhere far off, a source of strength sufficiently distant to leave his sensitivity lucid, not perturbed by too close a contact—a woman who was there for him, who did not expect more from him than his words, a sort of transformer, whose every technical fault he knew and mastered well enough to be able to rectify it at once by letter. The woman who thus served his purposes had not to be exposed to the influences of his family, from whose proximity Kafka suffered greatly: he had to keep her away from them. She would have to take seriously everything he had to say about himself. Sparing of words as he was in speech, in writing he would expatiate upon himself to her, set forth his complaints regardless: he must hold nothing back, since that might disconcert him in the act of writing; he must tell her, in every detail, of the importance, the continuance, and the hesitations of this writing. His diary stops during this period—the letters to Felice are his expanded diary, with the advantage that he really does write an entry each day, that here he can repeat himself more frequently and thus yield to an important need of his nature. What he writes to her are not unique things which are set down once and for all; he can correct himself in later letters, he can confirm or retract. And even volatility, which with his controlled intelligence he begrudges himself in the single diary entries, because he regards it as being disorderly, is quite possible in the sequence of the letters. But doubtless the chief advantage, as already indicated, is that repetitions, veritable litanies, are possible. If anyone was ever cognizant of the need and function of "litanies," it was Kafka. Among his very pronounced characteristics as a writer, it is this that has most often led to the "religious" misinterpretations of his work.

The opening of this correspondence was so important for Kafka that its effects continued to be felt by him for three months; further, it led to works as singular as *The Metamorphosis*. Why then does his writing suddenly come to a standstill in January 1913? Statements about a writer's having productive and unproductive periods would not answer this question adequately. Productivity always has its determinants, and one should make the effort to find out what causes productivity to stop.

Perhaps it should not be overlooked that the letters of the first period, though they can hardly be viewed as love letters in the usual sense, do entail an element that pertains quite especially to love: for Kafka it is important that Felice *expects* something of him. At the first meeting, from which he drew sustenance for such a long time, he had the manuscript of his first book with him. Felice had made his acquaintance as a writer, not merely as the friend of a writer whose work she knew somewhat; and Kafka's claim to receive letters from her is based on the premise that she regards him as such. The first story with which he is satisfied, "The Judgment," is *hers*; he is indebted to her for it, and he dedicated it to her. Naturally he is not sure about her literary opinions, and in his letters he tries to exert some influence on them. He asks for a list of the books she has, but he never receives one.

Felice was an uncomplicated person; this shows clearly enough in remarks of hers that are quoted in Kafka's letters. The dialogue that Kafka was conducting with himself by way of her—if such a standard word as dialogue can be applied to something so complex and subterranean—might have been continued for a long time. He, however, became bewildered by her craving for culture: she was reading other writers and named them in her letters. He had brought to light so far only a fraction of the tremendous world he felt to be in his head; and as a writer he wanted to have Felice for himself.

On December 11 he sends her his first book; *Meditation* has just been published. He writes: "Please be kind to my poor book! It consists of those few pages you saw me putting in order on our evening. . . . I wonder if you notice how the various pieces differ in age. One of them for example is certainly 8 to 10 years old. Show the book to as few people as possible, so as to avoid having your mind about me changed" (100).

On December 13 he mentions his book again: "I am so

happy to think that my book, no matter how much I find fault with it . . . is now in your possession" (104).

On December 23 the following lonely statement occurs: "Oh, if Frl. Lindner [a colleague of Felice's] only knew how difficult it is to write as little as I do!" (120). This alludes to the brevity of *Meditation* and can only be interpreted as a reply to an evasive remark in one of Felice's letters.

And that is all, until his great outburst of jealousy on December 28, seventeen days after he had sent her the book: the letters of that period, concerning matters of one kind and another, fill thirty closely printed pages, and, as has been noted, only his letters survive. It is evident that Felice expressed not a single serious opinion on *Meditation*. His outburst is now aimed against Herbert Eulenberg, about whom Felice is enthusiastic: "I am jealous of all the people in your letter, those named and those unnamed, men and girls, business people and writers (writers above all, needless to say). . . . I am jealous of Werfel, Sophocles, Ricarda Huch, Lagerlöf, Jacobsen. My jealousy is childishly pleased because you call Eulenberg Hermann instead of Herbert, while Franz no doubt is deeply engraved on your brain. (You like the *Silhouettes*? You find them pithy and clear?) 'Mozart' is the only one I know in its entirety, Eulenberg . . . gave a reading of it here, but I could hardly bear it, the breathless unclean prose. . . . But of course there is no doubt that in my present condition I am doing him a grave injustice. *But you ought not to read the* Silhouettes. And now I see that you are even 'very enthusiastic' about him. (Listen everyone: Felice is very enthusiastic about him, very enthusiastic indeed, and here am I raging against him in the middle of the night.) But other people are to be found in your letter as well; I want to start a fight with them all, the whole lot, not because I mean to do them any harm, but to drive them away from you, to get you away from them, to read only letters that are concerned solely with you, your family, . . . and of course, of course, me!" (129).

The following day he receives from her a letter that is unexpected, for it is Sunday, and he thanks her: "Dearest, once again this is the kind of letter that makes one go hot with silent joy. It is not full of all those friends and writers" (131).

That very night he finds an explanation for the previous day's jealousy: "By the way, now I know more precisely why yesterday's letter made me so jealous: You don't like my book any more than you liked my photograph. This really wouldn't matter, for what is written there is largely old stuff. . . . I feel your presence so acutely in everything else that I should be quite prepared . . . to be the *first* to kick the little book aside with *my* foot. . . . But why don't you tell me, tell me in two words, that you don't like it! It would be quite understandable if you did not like the book. . . . No one will know what to make of it, that is and was perfectly clear to me; the trouble the spendthrift publisher took and the money he lost, both utterly wasted, prey on my mind too. . . . But you said nothing, or rather you did once announce that something would be said, but did not say it" (132).

At the end of January he comes back to *Meditation:* the Viennese writer Otto Stoessl, whom he rates highly and likes personally, has written him a letter about it: "He also writes about my book, but with such complete lack of understanding that for a moment I thought the book must really be good, since—even in a man as discerning and experienced in literary matters as Stoessl—it can create the kind of misunderstanding one would consider impossible with books" (177). He copies for her the whole relevant section of the letter, which is fairly lengthy. There are astounding remarks in it: "It is full of very pertinent humor, turned inward as it were, not unlike the way in which, after a good night's sleep, a refreshing bath, and dressed in clean linen, one welcomes a free, sunny day with happy expectations and an inconceivable sensation of strength. The humor of a healthy frame of mind" (178). A mistake of monstrous proportions, every word utterly wrong; Kafka boggles at the phrase "humor of a healthy frame of mind," and later he quotes it again. But he also adds: "The letter, incidentally, goes rather well with an extravagantly favorable review published today, which finds in the book nothing but sorrow" (178).

It is clear that he has not forgotten her disregard of *Meditation;* the amplitude of his account of Stoessl's reactions—unusual for Kafka—covers a wound. He wants to teach Felice a lesson—she has made things too easy for herself—and he thereby betrays how hurt he has been by her failure to react.

The most violent outburst against another writer comes during the first half of February. Felice has asked him about Else Lasker-Schüler, and he writes: "I cannot bear her poems; their emptiness makes me feel nothing but boredom, and their contrived verbosity nothing but antipathy. Her prose I find just as tiresome and for the same reasons; it is the work of an indiscriminate brain twitching in the head of an overwrought city-dweller. . . . Yes, she is in a bad way; I believe her second husband has left her; they are collecting for her here, too; I have to give 5 kronen, without feeling the slightest sympathy for her. I don't quite know why, but I always imagine her simply as a drunk, dragging herself through the coffeehouses at night. . . . Away with you,

Lasker-Schüler! Come here, dearest! No one is to be between us, no one around us" (191).

Felice plans a visit to the theater to see Arthur Schnitzler's *Professor Bernhardi*, and Kafka writes: "But if you go to *Professor Bernhardi*, dearest, you drag me along by that inevitable cord, and there is a danger that we both succumb to that kind of bad literature, which the greater part of Schnitzler represents for me" (193). So he goes, the same evening, to see *Hidalla*, in which Frank Wedekind and his wife are playing: "For I don't like Schnitzler at all, and hardly respect him; no doubt he is capable of certain things, but for me his great plays and his great prose are full of a truly staggering mass of the most sickening drivel. It is impossible to be too hard on him. . . . Only when looking at his photograph—that bogus dreaminess, that sentimentality I wouldn't touch even with the tips of my fingers—can I see how he could have developed in this way from his partly excellent early work (*Anatol*, *La Ronde*, *Lieutenant Gustl*). —Wedekind I won't even mention in the same letter.

"Enough, enough! Let me quickly get rid of Schnitzler who is trying to come between us, like Lasker-Schüler the other day" (193).

His jealousy of other writers, as far as Felice's interest in them is concerned, is just as strong as jealousy usually is; one is astonished and relieved to find Kafka being so naturally, wholeheartedly aggressive toward others. Throughout these numerous letters one can hear the better-known voice of the Kafka who is aggressive toward himself. Yet the unusual tone of these attacks on other writers, who are actually worlds apart from him, the murderous quality of the attacks, their crassness, are symptomatic of a change in his relationship with Felice. This change takes a tragic turn because of her failure to understand his writing. He needs her strength, as a steady flow of sustenance for his work; yet she is not capable of comprehending who it is that she is sustaining with her letters.

His situation, in this regard, is all the worse because of the nature of his first book. He is too sensible and too serious to overestimate the weight of *Meditation*. It is a book that announces many of his themes. But it is patchwork, still rather moody and artistic; it shows extraneous influences (Robert Walser), and it lacks, quite particularly, unity and urgency. For him it has significance because he had the manuscript with him when he first saw Felice.

But six weeks after that evening, directly after his first letter to Felice, he has become entirely himself, in "The Judgment" and "The Stoker." Almost more important here is the fact that he was seemingly quite aware of the value of these two texts. The correspondence with Felice was beginning, night after night he was writing his things, and after eight weeks, in *The Metamorphosis*, he is at the height of his mastery. He had written something he would never surpass, because there is nothing that could possibly surpass *The Metamorphosis*, one of the few great and perfect works of poetic imagination written during this century.

Four days after the completion of *The Metamorphosis, Meditation* is published. He sends this first book to Felice and waits seventeen days for a word about it from her. Letters are exchanged several times a day; he waits in vain and has already written *The Metamorphosis* and a large part of *Amerika*. It is enough to wring tears from a stone: he now realized that the sustenance given by her letters, without which he could not write, had been given blindly. His doubts, always present, became overwhelming; he was no longer certain of his claim to the letters he had extracted from her during the good time. And his writing, which was his very life, began to falter.

An indirect—but in its violence very striking—result of this catastrophe was his jealousy of other writers. Felice wounded him deeply with names of authors she was reading, names that kept coming up in her letters. In her eyes, all these were *Dichter* [poets, writers]. But what, in her eyes, was he?

The blessings she had bestowed upon him thus came to an end. With his immense tenacity, the astounding reverse side of his frailty, he held fast to the form of the existing relationship, and from that standpoint looked longingly back upon the paradise of those three months that could never return. The equilibrium she had given him had been destroyed.

Certainly during those days other occurrences had contributed to this disturbance. There was, for instance, the engagement of Max Brod, his best friend, who, more than anyone else, had urged him and goaded him to write. Kafka is afraid of the change in this relationship, made inevitable merely by the wife's presence, so it seemed. During this time too there were the preparations for his sister Valli's wedding; all that this involved he experienced at first hand in his parents' home, which was also his. It makes him sad to think that his sister will be leaving, he feels that the family is crumbling away—yet he also hates the family. But he has accommodated himself in this hatred and he needs it. The many unfamiliar events which fill an entire month before the wedding are disturbing to him. He wonders why he suffers in this strange way from these betrothals, as if some immediate sudden misfortune were assailing him, while the chief participants themselves are unexpectedly fortunate and happy.

His aversion to marriage as a way of life, marriage for which such ample preparations had been made, is now more pronounced than before. He gives free rein to this contrary reaction whenever people might be expecting this way of life from him: he begins to sense that Felice is a danger to him; his solitary nights are threatened, and he lets her feel this.

But before his attempts to guard against this danger are discussed, we must be more precise about the way in which he felt threatened.

"My mode of life is devised solely for writing. . . . Time is short, my strength is limited, the office is a horror, the apartment is noisy, and if a pleasant, straightforward life is not possible then one must try to wriggle through by subtle maneuvers" (21–22). Thus Kafka wrote in an early letter, his ninth to Felice, dated November 1, 1912. He goes on to explain to her how he has begun to arrange his time, with the result that he can settle down to his writing at 10:30 every night, and work until 1:00, 2:00, or 3:00 in the morning, according to his strength, inclination, or luck.

Yet even prior to this, in the same letter, he has made a remark about himself which is quite staggering in this context: "I am the thinnest person I know (and that's saying something, for I am no stranger to sanatoria)" (21). This man, asking for love—one does after all suppose that such is the case—starts off by calling himself the thinnest of men! Why, actually, does such a statement seem so inappropriate at this stage, even almost culpable? Love is a matter of weight, bodies are involved; bodies have to be there, it is ridiculous if a nonbody asks for love. Great suppleness, spirits, impetus—all can substitute for weight, but they must be active, present themselves, be a constant promise, as it were. Kafka, instead, comes forward with what is peculiarly his own: the fullness of what he has seen, seen of the appearance of the person being wooed. This fullness is *his* body. Yet this could only be appreciated by someone with a like fullness of visual experience; anyone else would not notice it, or would find it weird.

This immediate and emphatic reference to his thinness can only mean that it was a cause of suffering to him: he feels compelled to speak of it. It is as if he were obliged to say "I am deaf" or "I am blind," because otherwise concealment would brand him as a deceiver.

One does not need to look far in his diaries and letters to become convinced that here one has grasped the core, the root, of Kafka's "hypochondria." The diary entry dated November 22, 1911, contains the following statement: "It is certain that a major obstacle to my progress is my physical condition. Nothing can be accomplished with such a body. . . . My body is too long for its weakness, it hasn't the least bit of fat to engender a blessed warmth, to preserve an inner fire, no fat on which the spirit could occasionally nourish itself beyond its daily need without damage to the whole. How shall the weak heart that lately has troubled me so often be able to pound the blood through all the lengths of these legs."[6]

On January 3, 1912, he gives a detailed account of what he has sacrificed on behalf of his writing: "When it became clear in my organism that writing was the most productive direction for my being to take, everything rushed in that direction and left empty all those abilities which were directed toward the joys of sex, eating, drinking, philosophical reflection, and above all music. I atrophied in all these directions. This was necessary because the totality of my strengths was so slight that only collectively could they even halfway serve the purpose of my writing."[7]

On July 17, 1912, writing to Max Brod from Jungborn, Kafka says: "I have the silly idea of fattening myself up, and going on from there to a general cure, as if the latter or even the former were possible."[8]

The next reference to his thinness comes in his letter to Felice dated November 1, 1912, already cited. A few months later, on January 10, 1913, he writes again to Felice: "What was it like at the mixed baths? Alas, this is where I have to suppress a remark (it refers to my appearance in the bath, my thinness). In the bath I look like an orphan" (152). Then he tells how as a small boy at a summer resort on the Elbe he had avoided the very small, crowded swimming area because he was ashamed of his appearance.

In September 1916, he decides to consult a doctor, a very unusual enterprise for him, since he distrusts doctors, and he writes Felice about the visit: "The doctor whom I went to see . . . was very pleasant. A quiet, rather funny man who nevertheless, by his age and physical bulk (how you could ever come to trust anything as long and thin as me is something I shall never understand)—as I was saying, by his bulk . . . inspired confidence" (499).

Let me cite several more passages from the last seven years of his life, after he had ended his relationship with Felice. It is important to note that this idea of his thinness retained its potency in him to the end, and colored all his memories.

In the famous "Letter to His Father," written in 1919, there is another reference to childhood swimming: "I remember, for instance, how we often undressed in the same bathing hut. There was I, skinny, weakly, slight; you strong, tall, broad. Even inside the hut I felt a miserable specimen, and what's more, not only in your eyes but in the eyes of the whole world, for you were to me the measure of all things."[9]

Most striking is the reference in one of his earliest letters to Milena Jesenská in 1920.[10] Here, too, he feels compelled, during an early stage of his wooing a woman—and he wooed Milena with a passion—to present himself to her in all his thinness: "Several years ago I often used to go in a man-drowner [small boat] on the Moldau, I rowed upstream and then, stretched out on my back, floated downstream with the current, under the bridge. Because of my extreme thinness this may have looked very funny from the bridge. The clerk, having once seen me from the bridge like this and having sufficiently emphasized the humorous aspect, summarized his impressions as follows: It looked like a scene just before the Last Judgment, like the moment when the lids had already been lifted from the coffins, but the dead were still lying motionless."[11]

The figures of the thin man and the dead man are seen as one: with these allied to the idea of the Last Judgment, there emerges an image of his corporeality that could hardly be more forlorn and fraught with doom. It is as if the thin man, or the dead man, who are one here, had just enough life in them to let themselves drift downstream, and to surrender to the Last Judgment.

During the last weeks of his life in the sanatorium at Kierling, Kafka had been advised by his doctors not to speak. He answered questions in writing, on slips of paper that have been preserved. Once he was asked about Felice, and he wrote the following answer: "Once I was supposed to go to the Baltic coast with her and a friend of hers, but I was ashamed because of my thinness and general fearfulness."

Kafka never lost his pronounced sensitivity to anything that related to his body. This sensitivity, as the foregoing utterances show, must have marked even his childhood. Early on, his thinness made him attentive to his body. He became accustomed to taking note of anything that his body lacked. He had found, in his body, an object of observation which never escaped him, which could not slip away from him. What he saw of it, and felt, was always close to him: the one could not be dissociated from the other. With his thinness as starting-point, he became unshakably convinced of his frailty; and perhaps it is not so very important to know whether or not such frailty was always the case. For the one certain thing was a feeling, based on this conviction, of being threatened. He is afraid that alien forces will penetrate his body; and to forestall this he studies vigilantly the course they might take. Gradually thoughts about the individual organs beset him. A pronounced sensitivity to these organs begins to develop, until finally each is placed under a separate guard. But by this the dangers are multiplied—there are countless symptoms to be watched by a mind fraught with suspicion, once that mind is aware of the special character of the organs and of their vulnerability. There are moments of pain, here or there, and they bring those organs back to mind; it would be arrogant and culpable to ignore them. The pains warn of dangers, they are heralds from the adversary. Hypochondria is the small change of *Angst;* it is *Angst* which, for its distraction, seeks names and finds them.

His sensitivity to noise is like a warning; it announces ancillary, as yet unarticulated dangers. One can evade these by avoiding noise like the devil: he has enough to do with the recognized dangers, whose concerted attacks he repulses, by *naming* them.

His room is a shelter, it becomes an outer body, one can call it his "forebody": "I have to sleep alone; you may take this for courage, actually it is apprehension: just as when lying on the floor one cannot fall, so, when alone, nothing can happen to one" (176). Visitors in his room are intolerable to him. Even living together with his family in one apartment is a torment: "I cannot live with people; I absolutely hate all my relatives, not because they are my relatives, not because they are wicked . . . but simply because they are people with whom I live in close proximity" (287).

Most of all he complains about sleeplessness. Perhaps sleeplessness is simply vigilance over the body and cannot be switched off, keeps detecting threats, waiting for signals, which it interprets and combines, inventing systems of countermeasures and working toward a point at which those systems are secured: the point at which the threats balance one another out, the point of rest. Sleep then becomes a real liberation—sleep, in which the insomniac's sensitivity, this unceasing torment, finally lets him go, and disappears. There is, in Kafka, a sort of sleep-worship; he regards sleep as a panacea. The best thing he can recommend to Felice whenever her state of mind troubles him is "Sleep! Sleep!" Even the reader heeds this exhortation as a magical charm, a benediction.

Included among the threats to the body are all the poisons that enter it—as breath, as food and drink, as medicines.

Bad air is dangerous. Kafka often writes of this. One only has to think of the attic offices in *The Trial*, or of the painter Titorelli's overheated studio. Bad air is felt to be bad luck, and it leads to the brink of catastrophe. Kafka's travel diaries are full of the cult of good air: his letters show what expectations he had of it. He sleeps, even on the coldest winter nights, with the window open. Smoking is forbidden; heating uses up the air—he writes in an unheated room. He does regular physical exercises at an open window. His body offers itself to the fresh air, so that it can flow over skin and pores. But the true air is out in the country; the country life is something he encourages his favorite sister, Ottla, to try, and later he makes it his own way of life for months on end.

He seeks out food he is convinced is not harmful. For long periods his diet is vegetarian. Initially this régime does not really seem to be ascetic; in reply to an anxious query from Felice, he sends her a list of the fruits he chooses from in the evening. He seeks to fend off poisons and dangers from his body. As a matter of course he has forbidden himself coffee, tea, and alcohol.

There is something like levity and exuberance in his statements when he writes about this aspect of his life, whereas despair always speaks in his accounts of sleeplessness. This contrast is so striking that one feels tempted to elucidate it. He is attracted to what the practitioners of natural healing recommend, because of their conception of the body as a unity; he concurs wholeheartedly in their rejection of therapy for particular organs. During his own bouts of sleeplessness he himself disintegrates into his separate organs, he waits for signals from them, he considers their ominous stirrings; and so he needs a method that prescribes unity for his body. Official medicine seems to him harmful, because it is overmuch concerned with the separate organs. In his rejection of medicine there is, of course, a certain amount of self-hatred: he, too, when he lies sleepless at night, is in search of symptoms.

Thus he plunges with a sort of elation into every activity that demands and restores unity of the body. Swimming, exercising naked, leaping wildly up the stairs at home, running, long walks in the country which enable him to breathe freely—all these enliven him and give him hope that for once, or even for a longer time, he might be able to escape from the disintegration of the wakeful night.

Toward the end of January 1913, after repeated attempts to continue it, Kafka finally gave up writing his novel *Amerika;* and so the accent in his letters now tends to land more and more on complaint. One is tempted to say that hereafter the letters are in the service of complaint. There is nothing left to balance his dissatisfaction; the night during which he found himself, his justification, his one true life —these now belong mainly to the past. Only complaint holds him together; it takes the place of writing as his integrating factor—a much less valuable one—but without it he would become speechless, in the fragmentations of pain. He has become accustomed to the freedom of the letters, in which he can say everything he pleases; here at least the taciturnity that afflicted him in the company of people has become less rigid. He needs the letters from Felice, who tells him, as before, about her life in Berlin; and if he has no fresh word from her to hang on to, it is for him like being "surrounded by a void" (217). For in spite of the insecurity that "follows my not writing like an evil spirit" (159), he does still remain for himself an object of observation. And once the reader has learned to read the litany of complaint as a sort of language into which everything else has been brought for shelter, he realizes that in this medium, a continuously expressive one, highly remarkable statements are being made about Kafka, with a precision and truth granted to few other writers.

The degree of intimacy in these letters baffles imagination: they are more intimate than any complete description of happiness might be. There is no other account of hesitancy to compare with this one; no other self-revelation has such fidelity. For a primitive person this correspondence would be almost unreadable; he would think it a shameless display of psychic impotence: for it is all here—the indecisiveness, the fearfulness, coldness of feeling, detailed description of lovelessness, a helplessness so vast that only excessively exact description makes it believable. Yet it is all so composed as to become, instantaneously, law and knowledge. Somewhat incredulous at first, but with rapidly increasing assurance, one finds that none of it can ever again be forgotten, as if it were written, as in "In the Penal Colony," on one's own skin. There are writers, admittedly only a few, who are so entirely themselves that any utterance one might presume to make about them must seem barbarous. Franz Kafka was such a writer; accordingly one must adhere as closely as possible to his own utterances, with the risk that one might seem slavish. Certainly one feels diffident as one begins to penetrate the intimacy of these letters. But the letters themselves take one's diffidence away. For, while reading them, one realizes that a story like *The Metamorphosis* is even more intimate than they are; and one comes at last to know what makes it different from all other stories.

The important thing about Felice was that she did exist,

that she was not invented, and that, the way she was, she could not have been invented by Kafka. She was so different, so active, so compact. As long as he was circling her from a distance he idolized and tormented her. His questions, his requests, his fears, his tiny hopes he heaped upon her, in order to force letters out of her. The love that she turned upon him flowed through his heart like blood, so he declared in one letter, and he had no other blood. He asked whether she had not noticed that, in his letters, he did not really love her, for, if he did, he would have to think only of her and write about her. As it was, he worshiped her, and he expected help and blessings from her for the most absurd things: "There are times, Felice, when I feel you have so much power over me that I think you could change me into a man capable of doing the obvious" (197). In a good moment he thanks her: "What a lovely feeling to be in your safekeeping when confronted by this fearful world which I venture to take on only during nights of writing" (249).

He feels that the other person's slightest wound has been inflicted upon himself. His cruelty is that of the noncombatant, who feels the wound *in advance.* He fearfully avoids confrontation, everything cuts into *his* flesh, and the enemy goes unharmed. If some remark in a letter might offend Felice, he draws her attention to it in the next one he writes, forcibly, and he reiterates his apology; but she doesn't notice anything, she does not even know, for the most part, what he is talking about. Thus in his way he treated her like an adversary.

He succeeds in epitomizing the character of his indecisiveness: "Have you ever observed how, within yourself and independent of other people, diverse possibilities open up in several directions, thereby actually creating a ban on your every movement?" (185).

The significance of these different possibilities, which open in this or that direction, and the fact that he sees them all simultaneously cannot be overestimated. They elucidate his actual relation to the future. For a good part of his work consists of tentative steps toward perpetually changing possibilities of future. He does not acknowledge a single future, there are many; this multiplicity of futures paralyzes him and burdens his step. Only when he is writing, when he approaches one of these futures hesitantly, does he focus his gaze on it and exclude the others; but never can more be seen of it than what the next step permits. His actual art consists thus in the concealment of distance. Probably it is this progression in one direction, detachment from other directions which might have been possible, that makes him happy while he is writing. The measure of achievement is the onward motion itself, the distinctness of the steps that succeed, none being omitted, none, once taken, remaining in doubt. "Nor can I tell a story properly; in fact I can hardly even talk; when I am telling a story I usually have the kind of feeling small children probably experience when attempting their first steps" (270).

He repeatedly complains about his difficulties in talking, his taciturnity in company with people, and he describes these difficulties with uncanny clarity: "Wasted another evening with various people. . . . I bit my lips to stop my attention from wandering, yet in spite of all my efforts I wasn't there at all, but was definitely nowhere else, either; so perhaps I didn't exist at all during those two hours? That must be it, for my presence would have been more convincing had I been asleep in my chair" (200). "I really do believe I am lost to all social intercourse" (271). He even goes so far as to maintain, surprisingly, that on all the journeys for weeks on end with Max Brod, he had never had a single long coherent conversation with him involving his entire being.

"I am at my most bearable in familiar surroundings with 2 or 3 friends; then I am free, am not forced to be continually attentive and cooperative, but can take part in what's going on if and when I feel like it, as much or as little as I wish; no one misses me, no one is made uneasy by my presence. If there is a stranger present who happens to get under my skin, all the better, for then, on borrowed strength, I seem to be able to become quite animated. But if I am in an unfamiliar place, among a number of strange people, or people whom I feel to be strangers, then the whole room presses on my chest and I am unable to move" (271).

He always turns such descriptions against himself as warnings, and, numerous as they are, he keeps reformulating them: "The trouble is, I am not at peace with myself; I am not always 'something,' and if for once I am 'something,' I pay for it by 'being nothing' for months on end" (213). He likens himself to a bird that, kept away from its nest by some kind of curse, keeps flying around the nest, which is totally empty, and never loses sight of it.

"I am now a different person to the one I was during the first 2 months of our correspondence; it is not a transformation into a new state, rather a relapse into an old and no doubt lasting one" (212). "My present state . . . is not an exceptional state. Don't succumb, Felice, to these misapprehensions! Not for 2 days could you live beside me" (215). "After all, you are a girl, and want a man, not a flabby worm of the earth" (211).

One of the countermyths he has set up for his own protection, seeking to prevent physical proximity and Felice's intrusion into his life, is the one that involves his aversion to children.

"I shall never have a child," he writes, early in the correspondence, on November 8 (32); but he still says it in terms of envy directed toward one of his sisters, who has just given birth to a girl. The matter becomes more serious at the end of December, when his disappointment with Felice mounts in increasingly somber and hostile letters written over a period of four nights. We know the first of these: it is his outburst of jealousy vis-à-vis Eulenberg; also the second, in which he reproaches Felice for not responding to his book *Meditation*. In the third he quotes from a collection of Napoleon's sayings: "It is terrible to die childless." He adds: "And I have to be prepared to take this upon myself, for . . . I would never dare expose myself to the risk of being a father" (134). In the fourth letter, written on New Year's Eve, he feels lost as a dog and describes almost spitefully the New Year's noise on the street. Then, at the end of the letter, he replies to a statement of hers—"we belong together unconditionally"—that this is true a thousand times over, and that no greater and crazier wish could be his, during the first hours of the new year, "than that we should be bound together inseparably by the wrists of your left and my right hand. I don't quite know why this should occur to me; perhaps because a book on the French Revolution, with contemporary accounts, is lying in front of me, and it may be possible after all . . . that a couple thus bound together were once led to the scaffold.—But what is all this that's racing through my head? . . . That's the 13 in the new year's date [bringing such thoughts]" (136–37).

Marriage as a scaffold—this was the notion with which he began the new year. It did not change throughout the year, despite all vacillations and events to the contrary. For him, the most tormenting thing about his notion of marriage must have been its ruling out the possibility of one's ever becoming so small as to be able to vanish: one has to be there. Fear of a superior power is central to Kafka, and his mode of resistance to such a power is transformation into something small. The consecration of places and of states of mind, which operates so astonishingly with him that one feels it is compulsive, is neither more nor less than a consecration of man. Every place, every moment, every trait, every step is serious and important and peculiar to itself. On the other hand, violation, which is unjust, is something that one must avoid by removing oneself as far from it as possible. One becomes very small, or one changes oneself into an insect, in order to save others from the guilt they incur by lovelessness and killing; one "denies oneself all hunger" for the others, who with their disgusting behavior refuse to leave one alone. But no situation is less favorable to this withdrawal than marriage. One must always be there, whether one wants it or not, for part of the day and part of the night—one's own magnitude corresponding to that of one's partner, a magnitude which may not change; otherwise it would be no marriage at all. But the place of smallness, which exists even in marriage, is usurped by the children.

One Sunday he is exposed to the "insane, monotonous, incessant shouting, singing, and hand-clapping" with which his father amuses, during the forenoon, a great-nephew, and in the afternoon a grandson (202). Tribal dances are more intelligible to him. But perhaps, he thinks, it is not just the shouting that puts such a strain on him; "altogether it requires strength to tolerate children in the apartment. I can't do it, I can't forget myself, my blood refuses to flow, it becomes congealed" (202), and it is this "desire of the blood" that represents itself as love for children.

Thus it is really envy that Kafka feels in the presence of children, but envy of a kind different from that which might be expected: an envy coupled with disapproval. At first children seem to be usurpers of smallness, the smallness into which he would like to slip. But it turns out that they are not actually small beings who want to disappear as he wants to. They are the false smallnesses, exposed to the noise and unpleasant influences of the adults—smallness goaded into becoming bigger, and also wanting just that, the very opposite of his deepest natural tendency, which is to become smaller, quieter, lighter, until one disappears.

If one does try to find what possibilities for happiness, or at least for well-being, he might have had, one is almost surprised to find—after all the testimonies of despondency, of numbness, and of failure—some that have force and are definite.

Above all, there is the solitude of writing. In the midst of writing *The Metamorphosis,* in his moment of greatest achievement, he asks Felice not to write him letters in bed at night, but rather to sleep. She should leave nocturnal writing to *him,* this small possibility of pride in his nightly work; and as proof of the fact that night work is everywhere, even in China, the man's prerogative, he transcribes for her a little Chinese poem, of which he is particularly fond. A scholar is so engrossed in his book that he has forgotten to go to bed. His mistress, who till now has restrained her anger with difficulty, snatches his lamp away and asks him, "Do you know how late it is?" (59–60).

That is how he sees his nightly work, as long as it is going well, and in quoting the poem he is not yet aware of any edge against Felice. Later, on January 14, when the situation has changed, Felice having disappointed him and his writing now on the verge of faltering, he remembers the Chinese scholar. But now the scholar is used to mark a frontier between himself and Felice: "You once said you would like to sit beside me while I write. Listen, in that case I could not write. . . . For writing means revealing oneself to excess. . . . This is why one can never be alone enough when one writes, why there can never be enough silence around one when one writes, why even night is not night enough. This is why there is never enough time at one's disposal, for the roads are long and it is easy to go astray. . . . I have often thought that the best mode of life for me would be to sit in the innermost room of a spacious locked cellar with my writing things and a lamp. Food would be brought and always put down far away from my room, outside the cellar's outermost door. The walk to my food, in my dressing gown, through the vaulted cellars, would be my only exercise. I would then return to my table, eat slowly and with deliberation, then start writing again at once. And how I would write! From what depths I would drag it up!" (155–56).

One should read the whole of this splendid letter; never has there been such a pure and severe statement about writing. All the ivory towers in the world crumble before this cellar-dweller; and the abused, emptied expression—"the solitude" of the writer—suddenly takes on weight and significance again.

This happiness, to which he is drawn by every fiber of

his being, is the only kind that has validity for him. A second and quite different situation which brings him gratification is that of the bystander observing the joy of other persons who leave him out and expect nothing of him. Thus, for instance, he enjoys being among people who are eating and drinking everything that he denies himself. "If I am sitting at a table with 10 friends all drinking black coffee, the sight of it gives me a feeling of happiness. Meat can be steaming around me, mugs of beer drained in huge drafts, those juicy Jewish sausages . . . can be cut up by every relative all over the place . . . —all this and worse gives me no sensation of distaste whatever; on the contrary, it does me a great deal of good. There is no question of my taking a malicious pleasure in it . . . it is rather a calm, a calm without envy at the sight of other people's delight" (163).

Perhaps these two situations of well-being are the ones one would expect of him, even though the second is more strongly emphasized than one would have expected. It is really surprising, however, to find that he is vouchsafed the happiness of *expansion,* in reading aloud. There is always a changed tone in his letters when he tells Felice that he has read some of his work aloud. He, who cannot weep, has tears in his eyes after reading "The Judgment." The letter of December 4, written immediately after this reading, is positively astonishing in its wildness: "Frankly, dearest, I simply adore reading aloud; bellowing into the audience's expectant and attentive ear warms the cockles of the poor heart. And bellow I certainly did, simply blowing away the music from adjoining rooms that was trying to spare me the trouble of reading aloud. Nothing, you know, gives the body greater satisfaction than ordering people about, or at least believing in one's ability to do so" (86). A few years earlier, he says, he had enjoyed dreaming of reading in a large, crowded hall the whole of Flaubert's *Education sentimentale*, a book that he loved most passionately, without interruption for as many days and nights as it might take to read aloud in French—and "making the walls reverberate" (86).

It is not, to be sure, a question of "ordering people about"—Kafka does not express himself quite accurately here, because of his exaltation: it is the *law* that he wishes to proclaim, a law at last assured; and if it just happens to be Flaubert, then for Kafka it is like the law of God and he would be Flaubert's prophet. But he also feels liberated and elated by this kind of expansion; in the midst of his misery in February and March he suddenly tells Felice: "A pleasant evening at Max's. I read myself into a frenzy with my story [probably the last part of *The Metamorphosis*]. But then we did let ourselves go, and laughed a lot. If one bolts the doors and windows against the world, one can from time to time create the semblance and almost the beginning of the reality of a beautiful life" (209).

Toward the end of February Kafka received from Felice a letter that alarmed him—it is as if he had never written her a word of self-denigration, as if she had not heard or believed or understood anything. He does not go at once into the question she asks, but later he replies with unusual abruptness: "The other day . . . you asked me about my plans and prospects. I was amazed by your question. . . . Needless to say I have no plans, no prospects; I cannot step into the future; I can crash into the future, grind into the future, stumble into the future, this I can do; but best of all I can lie still. Plans and prospects, however—honestly, I have none; when things go well, I am entirely absorbed by the present; when things go badly, I curse even the present, let alone the future!" (209).

It is a rhetorical answer, not a precise one, as is shown by his quite unbelievable way of describing his relationship to the future. In a panic, he takes a defensive attitude. Several months later one meets with other rhetorical outbursts of this kind; they contrast very sharply with the just and balanced mode of his statements generally.

But after this letter the idea of visiting Berlin, an idea he had begun to entertain a few weeks earlier, starts to assume a more solid shape. He wishes to see Felice again, to frighten her away by appearing in person, since his letters have failed to do so. He chooses Easter for his visit, having two days free at that time. The way in which he announces his visit is so typical of his indecisiveness that some passages must be quoted from these letters of the week before Easter. It is the first time for more than seven months that they will be seeing each other; actually it will be their first meeting since that one evening.

On March 16, the Sunday before Easter, he writes: "A point-blank question, Felice: At Easter, that is, Sunday or Monday, would you have any one hour to spare for me, and if so, would you consider it a good thing if I came?" (224).

On Monday he writes: "I don't know if I shall be able to come. It is still uncertain today, tomorrow it may be definite" (224–25).

On Tuesday: "*Strictly speaking* the obstacle to my journey still exists and I'm afraid will continue to exist; but it has lost its significance as an *obstacle*; so, as far as that goes, I

could come. I just wanted to tell you this in haste, dearest"
(226).

On Wednesday: "I am going to Berlin for no other
reason than to tell and show you—you who have been
misled by my letters—who I really am. Shall I be able to
make it clearer in person than I could in writing? . . . Where
can I meet you then on Sunday morning? However, should
I still be prevented from coming, I would send a telegram
on Saturday at the latest" (226).

On Thursday: "And in addition to the old threats,
newly emerging further threats of possible obstacles to my
short journey. Now at Easter there are usually—I hadn't
thought of it before—meetings of all kinds of societies"
(227). Perhaps he might have to attend such a congress as
the representative of his insurance company.

On Friday: "And besides it's not yet at all certain that I'll
come; it won't be decided until tomorrow morning. . . . If I
come, I shall most probably stay at the Askanische Hof. . . .
But before appearing before you I must have a proper
sleep" (227).

He mails this last letter on the morning of Saturday,
March 22. He sends a final message: "Still undecided." But
then, the same day, he catches the train to Berlin and arrives
there late in the evening.

On Easter Sunday, March 23, he writes from the Askanische Hof: "But what has happened, Felice? . . . Now I
am in Berlin, and will have to leave again this afternoon at 4
or 5; the hours are passing, and no word from you. Please
send your answer with the boy. . . . I am sitting at the
Askanische Hof—waiting" (228).

Understandably enough, Felice's belief that he would
come had been shaken by the week's conflicting an-

nouncements. For about five hours he lay on the couch in his hotel room, waiting for her uncertain call. She lived a good way off, yet eventually he did see her. She did not have much time; they met twice in all, for a few moments. That was their first meeting in more than seven months.

But Felice seems to have made good use even of these few moments. She takes all responsibility upon herself. She says that he has become indispensable to her. The important result of the visit is their decision to meet again at Whitsun. This time they were to be apart for only seven weeks, not seven months. One has the impression that Felice has now set them both a goal, and that she is trying to infuse into Kafka the power to reach a decision.

Fourteen days after his departure he surprises her with the news that he has been working for a gardener in a suburb of Prague, in the cool rain, wearing only a shirt and trousers. It has done him good. His main purpose is "to escape self-torture for a few hours—in contrast to my ghostly work at the office . . . to do some dull, honest, useful, silent, solitary, healthy, strenuous work" (238). In this way, he says, he wants to earn a somewhat better night's sleep. Shortly before this he enclosed a letter from Kurt Wolff for her to read, in which the latter asked if he could publish "The Stoker" and *The Metamorphosis.* It looks like a revival of his hope that she might appreciate him as a writer.

But on April 1 he had also written her a quite different letter, one of those counterletters he used to announce in advance in order to stress their finality: "My one fear— surely nothing worse can either be said or listened to—is that I shall never be able to possess you. . . . I would sit beside you and, as has happened, feel the breath and life of your body at my side, yet in reality be further from you than now, here in my room. . . . Though you might lean toward me far enough for you to be in danger, I would be excluded from you forever" (233). This letter suggests that he had fears of impotence; but one should not place too much stress on this, it must be understood as just one of his many physical fears, such as were discussed in detail above. Felice does not react, as if she does not understand at all what is meant, or as if she knows him now only too well to want to understand.

But during the ten days she works in Frankfurt arranging an exhibit for her firm, he receives scant news from her; postcards only, and a telegram from the trade center. From Berlin, after her return, she also writes less frequently and more briefly. Perhaps she has realized that this is the only way to influence him, and by her not writing she pushes him closer to the decision she expects from him. He is manifestly alarmed: "Your recent letters are different. My affairs are no longer as important to you, and what is much worse: you no longer bother to tell me about yourself" (247). He discusses with her the Whitsun journey. He wants to meet her parents, an important step. He entreats her not to meet him at the station, because he always arrives in a terrible state.

On May 11 and 12 he sees her again in Berlin. On this occasion he spends more time with her than at Easter, and he is received by her family. Shortly afterward, he writes that her family gave the appearance of being altogether resigned with regard to him: "I felt so very small while they all stood around me like giants with such fatalistic expressions on their faces. . . . It was entirely in keeping with the situation: you are theirs, so they are big, you are not mine, so I was small. . . . I must have made a very nasty impression on them" (257). The remarkable feature in this letter is the translation of the property and power relationships into terms of physical smallness and bigness. The small person as the powerless one is a figure familiar to us from his writings. The corresponding image is found here in the gigantic—and for him overpowering—members of the Bauer family.

Yet it is not only the family, in particular the mother, that terrifies and paralyzes him; he is also troubled about the nature of his influence on Felice herself: "You are not I, your nature is to act; you are energetic, quick-thinking, observant; I saw you at home . . . , I saw you among strangers in Prague, you were always sympathetic, yet sure of your-self—but when you are with me, you flag, turn your head or stare at the grass, endure the silly things I say as well as my many well-founded silences, do not seriously wish to know anything about me, but simply suffer, suffer, suffer" (256). No sooner is she alone with him than she begins to behave as he does: she is silent, she becomes uncertain and morose. It is, of course, probable that he mistook the reason for her uncertainty: she cannot seriously wish to hear anything that he has to say, for she knows what she would find out—fresh and very eloquent doubts, to which she can oppose nothing but her sim.ple resolve to become engaged. Moreover, it is noticeable how deeply his image of her is still determined by that one evening in Prague "among strangers." Perhaps now it will be realized why at the outset I discussed that first evening in such detail.

Yet, whatever new scruples may have arisen because of her behavior in his presence, he promises to write her father a letter which he will first send to her for her opinion of it. On May 16 he says that he will write it; again on May 18. On May 23 he specifies what will be in the letter, but it never arrives; he cannot contrive to write it. She meanwhile employs her only weapon, silence, and for ten days she leaves him without news. "A ghost of a letter" arrives, one that he complains about bitterly. He quotes from it: "We are all here, sitting in the restaurant at the zoo, after spending the entire afternoon at the zoo. I am now writing under the table, while discussing traveling plans for next summer" (264). He implores her to write as she was doing earlier: "Dearest Felice, please write and tell me about yourself, as in the old days, about the office, about your friends, your family, your walks, about books; you have no idea how important it is to my life" (265). He wants to know if "The Judgment" has any meaning for her. He sends her *The Stoker,* just published. Once she does write more fully, and this time she is in doubt about herself. He is preparing a "treatise" that she will have to answer, but it is not yet ready, and after this announcement from him her letters stop once more. On June 15, in despair at her silence, he writes: "What do I want from you? What makes me persecute you? Why don't I desist, or heed the signs? On the pretext of wanting to free you of me, I force myself upon you" (268–69). Then, on June 16, he does finally send her the "treatise," on which he has worked haltingly for an entire week. It is the letter in which he asks her to become his wife.

There never has been a more curious proposal of marriage. In it he compiles his difficulties; he says countless things about himself that stand in the way of a shared marital life, and he asks her to consider carefully all these things. In letters that follow he adds further difficulties. His own reluctance to share life with a woman is very clearly expressed in these letters. But it is equally clear that he is afraid of solitude and is thinking of the strength that another person's presence could give him. He sets fundamentally impossible conditions for marriage and counts on a refusal, which he desires and provokes. But he is also hoping for a strong, unerring feeling on her part, which will brush away all difficulties and take him in hand. As soon as she has consented, he realizes that he should not have left the decision to her. "I have not come to the end of my counterarguments, their list is endless" (293). He thinks over her consent, as if to save the appearances, and then accepts her as his "beloved bride. And promptly . . . but perhaps for the last time, I say that I am absurdly afraid of our future and of the unhappiness which, through my fault and temperament, could develop from our life together, and which would be bound to affect you first and the more profoundly, for I am basically a cold, selfish, callous creature, despite my weakness which conceals rather than mitigates these qualities" (293).

And now begins his unrelenting struggle against the engagement. This persists for the next two months and ends in flight. The passage just quoted characterizes this struggle. Whereas earlier he had given accounts of himself that were—one is inclined to say—straightforward, now his letters include more and more, as his panic increases, a rhetorical note. He pleads the case against himself like an advocate using all available means, and it cannot be denied that these means are sometimes ignominious. At his mother's request, a Berlin detective agency had provided information about Felice's reputation, and he then describes to her the "elaborate document, as gruesome as it is intensely funny. We shall laugh about it one day" (282). She seems to accept this quietly, perhaps because of the jolly tone, which she does not see through. But immediately thereafter, on July 3, his thirtieth birthday, he tells her that his parents have expressed a wish to have information about Felice's family too, and that he has given his consent to this. But this wounds Felice deeply. She loves her family. He defends his move with sophistical arguments, even his insomnia is brought in as an excuse. Although he by no means admits he is in the wrong, he asks her to forgive him, because he has hurt her feelings, and he withdraws permission from his parents to solicit information. This affair contradicts so sharply his character as we otherwise know it that it can only be explained by his panic fear of the engagement's consequences.

Whenever it is a question of saving himself from marriage, all he can muster is eloquence directed against himself. It can at once be recognized as such; its main feature is the disguising of his own fears as anxieties about Felice. "Haven't I for months now been squirming before you like something poisonous? Am I not here one moment, there the next? Are you not beginning to feel sick at the sight of me? Can you not see by now that if disaster—yours, your disaster, Felice—is to be averted, I have to remain locked up within myself?" (287-88). He asks her to *counteradvertise* against him with her father, even if it means showing her father his letters: "Be honest with your father, Felice, since I haven't been. Tell him who I am, show him some letters, with his help step out of the accursed circle into which, blinded by love as I was and am, I forced you with letters, pleas, and supplications" (309). The rhapsodic note here is almost like something from Franz Werfel; Kafka knew Werfel well and felt attracted to him, inexplicable as this may seem today.

There can be no doubt as to the authenticity of his torment; and when he leaves Felice out of the picture—she appears here as no more than a delusion—he says things about himself that go straight to one's heart. His insight into

47

his own sensibility and nature is pitiless and terrifying. From among his many statements I cite only one here, one that seems to me the most important and terrifying: he says that fear and indifference combined make up his deepest feeling toward human beings (294).

This would explain the uniqueness of his work, in which emotions hardly appear, though literature otherwise swarms with them, volubly and chaotically. If one thinks about it with a little courage, our world has indeed become one in which fear and indifference predominate. Expressing his own reality without indulgence, Kafka was the first to present the image of *this* world.

On September 2, after two months of continuously worsening torment, Kafka quite suddenly announces to Felice that he is pulling out. It is a long letter, written in both languages—that of rhetoric and that of insight. Her need is "the greatest human happiness" (315)—which means no such thing to him, and which he renounces in favor of his writing; he has learned the lesson from his models: "Of the four men I consider to be my true blood-relations (without comparing myself to them either in power or in range), Grillparzer, Dostoevski, Kleist, and Flaubert, Dostoevski was the only one to get married, and perhaps Kleist, when compelled by outer and inner necessity to shoot himself on the Wannsee, was the only one to find the right solution" (315-16). He is traveling, he says, on Saturday to Vienna for the International Congress for First Aid and Hygiene, will stay there probably until the following Saturday, then go on to the sanatorium at Riva, stay there, and perhaps take a short trip in northern Italy. She should use this time to find peace and quiet. For the sake of her peace of mind he will forego all letters from her. For the first time, he does not ask her to write. And he will not write proper letters to her, either. Perhaps out of tact he does not tell her that the congress in Vienna to which he really does want to go is the Zionist Congress: it is one year since they discussed traveling together to Palestine.

He spent difficult days in Vienna. The congress and the many people he saw were unbearable to him in his desolate state. He tried in vain to find composure by writing some entries in his diary, and he traveled on to Venice. A letter to Felice from Venice reiterates in a more decided way his refusal to stand by the engagement. Then followed the days in a Riva sanatorium, where he met "the Swiss girl."[12] He quickly came to know her: a love affair ensued, one that he never denied, despite his usual delicate discretion; it lasted no more than ten days. It seems to have freed him from his self-hatred for a time. For six weeks, between mid-September and the end of October, relations between Kafka and Felice were severed. He wrote no more letters—anything, at that time, rather than her insistence on the engagement. Hearing nothing from him, she sent her friend Grete Bloch to Prague, with the request that Grete mediate between them. With the entry of a third person, a new and very remarkable phase in the relationship now began.

As soon as Grete Bloch enters the scene, Kafka becomes divided. The letters he was writing to Felice the previous year he now directs to Grete. Now it is she about whom he wishes to know everything, and he asks the same old questions. He wants to be able to picture how she lives, her work, her office, her travels. He wants immediate replies to his letters; and since they sometimes arrive late, though only slightly, he asks her to follow a regular schedule, which of course she refuses to do. He is interested in questions of her health; he wants to know what books she reads. In some respects he has an easier time of it than he had with Felice. Grete Bloch is more flexible, more receptive, more passionate. So she follows his suggestions. Even if she does not read at once the book he recommends, she makes a note of it and comes back to it later. Although her way of life is less conducive to health and less orderly than Felice's, she still gives consideration to his advice in these matters; she discusses them in her letters and thus goads him into making more sharply defined suggestions. He is not allowed to feel that his influence is not having results. In these letters, Kafka is more certain of himself, more overbearing, one might be tempted to say, were not Kafka himself the case in point. Naturally, the abridged form of the earlier correspondence comes to him more easily than the original; it is a keyboard on which he has had ample practice. There is something playful about these letters—a very rare feature in the earlier ones—and quite undisguisedly he is asking for Grete's affection.

Yet there are two essential differences. He complains much less; he is almost sparing with complaints. Since Grete Bloch soon opens her heart to him, and tells him about her own difficulties, he is touched by her sadness and comforts her; she comes to be something of a fellow sufferer, eventually even an alter ego. He tries to instill into her his own aversions, to Vienna, for example, a city he has hated since his ill-starred week there during the previous summer, and to which he is sending his letters to her. He does everything he can to make her leave Vienna, and he succeeds. Nevertheless, she has the good fortune to be a very efficient businesswoman; at least he thinks that she is. It is the one trait she shares with Felice, and he can draw strength from it, as before.

The principal topic of these letters remains, all the same, Felice. Grete Bloch first appeared in Prague as her emissary. From the start, Kafka can openly discuss with her everything that touches on his own part in the affair. She skillfully keeps feeding the original source of his interest in her. In the very first talk between them, she tells him things about Felice that arouse his repugnance: the story of her dental treatment, for example, and later there will be more about the new gold-capped teeth. But she mediates also, if Kafka is in distress, and when nothing else avails she manages to make Felice send him a postcard or some other message. His gratitude increases his affection for Grete Bloch, but he gives her to understand that his interest in her is not only part and parcel of their shared relationship to Felice. His letters become progressively warmer, wherever Grete is concerned. But he is ironic and detached when describing Felice.

Precisely this distance which he achieves through the correspondence with Grete Bloch, and certainly too his conversations with a new friend, the writer Ernst Weiss, who hates Felice and counsels against marriage to her, serve to strengthen Kafka's self-will, so that once again he is wooing Felice. Now he is manifestly determined to go through with the engagement and marriage, and he fights for them with a singleness of purpose hardly creditable to him after his earlier conduct. He is certainly well aware of his guilt of the previous year, when, at the last moment, just before their engagement was to be announced, he suddenly dropped Felice and absconded to Vienna and Riva. In a long letter to Felice written at the turn of the year 1913–14, he also tells Felice about the Swiss girl and, simultaneously, he asks her, for a second time, to marry him.

Her resistance is no less tenacious than his wooing; after her experience with him, one could hardly hold this against her. But precisely this resistance makes him more certain and more stubborn. He suffers humiliation and painful reverses; since he can tell Grete Bloch about these, everything is described to her at once and in detail. A very considerable part of his self-torment turns into accusations against Felice. If one reads the letters—often written on the same day—to Grete and to Felice, one can have no doubts as to whom he loves. The expressions of love in letters to Felice sound false and untrustworthy; in the letters to Grete Bloch, one can feel their presence, mostly unspoken, but that much more authentic, between the lines.

For two and a half months Felice remains adamant and indifferent. All the painful things he said about himself the previous year he now receives back from her, reduced to her primitive statements. Mostly, however, she says nothing at all; during an unexpected visit to Berlin, on a walk in the Tiergarten, he experiences his deepest humiliation. He humbles himself before her "like a dog," but achieves nothing. The account of this humiliation and its effect on him, spread over several letters to Grete Bloch, is of significance even apart from the context of the engagement. It shows how deeply Kafka suffered when humiliated. Certainly it was his most peculiar gift—the ability to make himself small by transformation—but he used this gift to reduce the humiliations, and it was successful reduction that made his enjoyment possible. In this regard he is to be sharply distinguished from Dostoevski; in contrast, Kafka is the proudest of men. Since he is saturated with Dostoevski and often expresses himself in the latter's idiom, one is sometimes seduced into misunderstanding him on this question. He never sees himself as a worm without hating himself for it.

Then Felice became uncertain, due to the loss of her handsome brother, whom she admired, and who it seems left Berlin because of some embarrassing money matters and had to emigrate to America. Her defenses crumbled. Kafka at once sees his advantage, and after four more weeks he succeeds in coercing her into an engagement. At Easter 1914, in Berlin, they become unofficially engaged.

Writing to Grete Bloch about it immediately after his return to Prague, Kafka tells her: "I know of nothing I have ever done with such determination" (385). But there was something else, too, which he cannot wait to tell her: "Our relationship, which for me at least holds delightful and altogether indispensable possibilities, is in no way changed by my engagement or my marriage" (385). He repeats his request for a meeting with her, a meeting he had often pictured, preferably in Gmünd, midway between Prague and Vienna. Earlier he had thought that they could meet, only the two of them, on a Saturday evening in Gmünd and then return to their respective cities on the Sunday evening; now what he has in mind is a meeting together with Felice.

The warmth of his affection for Grete increases after the Easter engagement. Without her, he would never have brought the engagement about, and he knows this. She gave him the strength he needed, as well as detachment with regard to Felice. But now, having come this far, he finds Grete even more indispensable. His requests that their friendship continue take on a character that is, for Kafka, tempestuous. She asks him to return her letters, and he refuses. He clings to them, as if they were those of his betrothed. He, who in fact cannot endure anyone in his room and home, urges her to spend the winter in the apartment where he and Felice will be living. He entreats her to come to Prague and to travel with him to Berlin for the official engagement, in lieu of his father. He continues to be concerned about her most personal affairs, perhaps a little more intensely than before. She tells him that she has visited the Grillparzer Room in Vienna, something he had been pressing her to do for a long time. He thanks her for the news: "It was very kind of you to go to the museum. . . . I felt the need to know you had been to the Grillparzer Room and that thus a physical tie had also been established between me and the room" (404). She has a toothache; he responds with many solicitous questions, and he describes, in doing so, the effect on him of Felice's practically "entire mouthful of gold-capped teeth" (405): "To tell the truth, this gleaming gold (a really hellish luster for this inappropriate spot) so scared me at first that I had to lower my eyes at the sight of F.'s teeth. . . . After a time, whenever I could, I glanced at it on purpose . . . to torment myself, and finally to convince myself that all this is really true. In a thoughtless moment I even asked F. if it didn't embarrass her. Of course it didn't—fortunately. But now I have become almost entirely reconciled. . . . I now no longer wish these gold teeth gone, but that's not quite the right expression, for I actually never did wish them gone. It's rather that they now strike me as almost becoming, most suitable, and . . . a very definite, genial, ever-present, visually undeniable human blemish which brings me perhaps closer to F. than could a healthy set of teeth, also horrible in its way" (406).

Felice *with* all her faults, faults now visible to him—and there were others besides the gold-capped teeth—it was this Felice whom he wanted to be his wife. During the previous year he had revealed himself to her with all his own faults, in a most terrifying manner. He had not been able to frighten her away with this image of himself, but his truth had acquired such power over him that he ran away from it, and from Felice, to Vienna and Riva. There, in his solitude and in deepest misery, he met the Swiss girl and found that he was capable of love—although he had thought himself incapable of it. This shook the "construction" he had put upon himself, as he later called it. I believe that it now became also a question of pride for him to repair his failure and truly to make Felice his wife. But now he was finding, in Felice's resistance, the effects of his self-revelation. A balance could only be struck if he took her as his wife with all her faults, which he was inquisitively seeking out, as she took him to be her husband.

But it was not love, although he told her otherwise. During the course of his very hard struggle for Felice, there came into being his love for the woman without whom he could not have survived this struggle—Grete Bloch. The marriage would only be complete, to his thinking, if she were included. All his instinctive actions of the seven weeks between Easter and Whitsun tended in this direction. Certainly, too, he was hoping that Grete would assist him in the awkward external situations in which he would now find himself and which he feared. But a broader idea was also involved, namely, that a marriage which he felt to be a sort of duty, a moral accomplishment, could not succeed without love. Through the presence of Grete Bloch he would have brought into the marriage the love he felt for her.

In this regard it must be said that, for Kafka, who seldom felt free in conversation, love came into being through his written word. The three most important women in his life were Felice, Grete Bloch, and Milena Jesenká. His feelings for each of them came into being through letters.

So things turned out as he had expected: the official engagement in Berlin was a time of terror for Kafka. At the reception given by the Bauer family on June 1, 1914, despite the much-desired presence of Grete Bloch, he felt "tied hand and foot like a criminal. Had they sat me down in a corner bound in real chains, placed policemen in front of me and let me look on simply like that, it could not have been worse. And that was my engagement; everybody made an effort to bring me to life, and when they couldn't, to put up with me as I was."[13] Thus his diary entry a few days afterward. In a letter written to Felice almost two years later, he describes another terror of those days, one that he still felt in his bones; it was the occasion of his going with her "to buy furniture in Berlin for an official in Prague": "Heavy furniture which looked as if, once in position, it could never be removed. Its very solidity is what you appreciated most. The sideboard in particular—a perfect tombstone, or a memorial to the life of a Prague official—oppressed me profoundly. If during our visit to the furniture store a funeral bell had begun tolling in the distance, it wouldn't have been inappropriate" (462).

As early as June 6, a few days after that reception, he wrote from Prague a letter to Grete Bloch which sounds uncannily familiar to the reader of the previous year's correspondence: "Dear Fräulein Grete, yesterday was another of those days when I felt completely tied down, incapable of moving, incapable of writing you the letter that everything still alive within me urged me to write. At times —and for the moment you are the only one to know—I really don't know how I, being what I am, can bear the responsibility of marriage" (420).

But Grete Bloch's attitude to him had taken a decisive change. She was now living in Berlin, as he himself had wished, and there she did not feel as isolated as she had felt in Vienna. She had her brother, of whom she was very fond, and other people from earlier times as well, and she was seeing Felice. Her mission, in which she must have believed—the bringing about of the engagement—had been successfully completed. Yet until shortly before her move to Berlin she had been receiving Kafka's letters; she had responded to them, between Kafka and herself there were secrets concerning Felice, and certainly she had developed strong feelings for him. The dress she was to wear at the engagement was discussed in their letters; it is as if she were the betrothed. "Don't try to improve it," he wrote of her dress, "no matter what it's like, it will be viewed with the, yes, with the most affectionate eyes" (418). He wrote her this letter one day before his departure and the official engagement.

The engagement, at which she was definitely not the betrothed, must have come as a shock to Grete. Soon afterward, Kafka complained to her about there being still three months to go until the wedding, and she replied: "Surely you'll be able to survive another 3 months" (423). This statement alone—and one knows few enough of her statements—is sufficient proof of the jealousy from which she certainly was suffering. With Felice nearby, since she was now living in Berlin, she could not but feel especially guilty. She could only rid herself of this guilt by crossing to Felice's side. So now she suddenly became Kafka's adversary and began to watch suspiciously for signs indicating that his decision to marry might not be serious. But he continued to write letters to her, trustingly, and more and more he unloaded into his letters his fears about the approaching marriage to Felice. She began to urge him on; he defended himself with the old arguments of his hypochondria, and, since it was Grete to whom he was addressing himself, he put his case in a more convincing and collected way than in the previous year's letters to Felice. He succeeded in giving her the alarm, she warned Felice, and Kafka was summoned to Berlin to face the "tribunal."

The "tribunal" at the Askanische Hof hotel in July 1914 marks the point of crisis in Kafka's double relation to the two women. The breaking of the engagement—although everything in Kafka was moving in that direction—seems to have been imposed on him from outside. But it is as if he himself had selected the members of this court, preparing them as no accused has ever done. The writer Ernst Weiss, though not present at the tribunal, at least lived in Berlin. He had been Kafka's friend for seven months; together with his literary qualities, he brought to the friendship something of inestimable value to Kafka: his steadfast rejection of Felice. From the very beginning he had opposed the engagement. For the same length of time, Kafka had been seeking Grete's love. He had bewitched her with his letters and brought her more and more to his side. During the time between the private and the official engagement, his love letters were being written to her, not to Felice. This placed her in a bind, from which she could only extricate herself by an about-face which would make *her* judge his case. She placed into Felice's hands the points of the accusation; in Kafka's letters to her there were passages she had underlined in red. Felice brought to the "tribunal" her sister Erna, perhaps as a counterweight to her absent adversary, Ernst Weiss. The accusation, a hard and spiteful one, was brought forward by Felice herself; the scant records we have do not make it clear whether or not Grete Bloch then directly intervened. But she was there, and Kafka felt that she was the real judge. He did not say a word, did not defend himself, and the engagement fell to pieces, just as he had wished. He left Berlin and spent two weeks at the seaside with Ernst Weiss. In his diary he describes his numbness during the Berlin days.

Or one might quite well view it in retrospect as follows: Grete Bloch was trying, in this way, to prevent an alliance of which she was jealous. Kafka, it can also be said, with a kind of provident premonition had directed her toward Berlin and then, with his letters, induced in her a state of mind in which she, instead of he, found the strength to rescue him from the engagement.

But the manner of this break, its concentrated form as "tribunal"—which is what Kafka called it afterward—had an overwhelming effect on him. At the beginning of August his reaction begins to formulate itself. The trial, which had been proceeding for two years in letters between him and Felice, now changed into that other *Trial*, which everybody knows. It is the same trial, he had rehearsed it; he incorporated into it infinitely more than the letters alone reveal, but that should not deceive us as to the identity of the two trials. The strength he had sought in Felice was now given to him by the shock of the tribunal. Simultaneously, the world came to judgment: World War I had begun.

The repugnance with which he regarded the mass events accompanying the outbreak of war increased his strength. He did not have for his private and interior processes that disregard which distinguishes insignificant writers from writers of imagination. A person who thinks that he is empowered to separate his inner world from the outer one has no inner world from which something might be separable. But with Kafka the problem was that the weakness he suffered from—the occasional collapse of his vital powers—made possible only a very sporadic exfoliation and objectification of his "private" processes. To achieve the continuity that he thought indispensable, two things were needed: a very powerful, yet somehow still erroneous shock, like the "tribunal," which mobilized his agonizing passion for precision as a defense against attacks from outside; and a bond between the external hell of the world and his inner hell. This came about in August 1914. He himself acknowledged the connection, and in his own way he gave distinct expression to it.

II

Two decisive events in Kafka's life—events which he of all people would have wanted to keep especially private—had taken place in a way that was embarrassingly public: the official engagement in the Bauer family home on June 1, and, six weeks later, on July 12, 1914, the "tribunal" at the Askanische Hof, which led to the breaking of the engagement. It can be shown that the emotional substance of both events entered directly into *The Trial*, which Kafka began to write in August. The engagement becomes the arrest in the first chapter; the "tribunal" appears as the execution in the last.

Several passages in the diaries make this connection so clear that one need have no qualms about proving it. The integrity of the novel is not thereby affected. If there were any need to enhance the novel's significance, a knowledge of the letters to Felice would provide the means for doing so. Fortunately, there is no such need. In no way, however, do the following considerations, intrusive as they may be, subtract anything from the novel's ever-increasing mystery.

Joseph K. is arrested in a house that is well known to him. He is still in bed, anyone's most familiar and intimate place, when the arrest procedure begins. All the more incomprehensible, then, are the morning's events: first, an entirely unknown person standing in front of him, and then a second person informing him that he is under arrest. This information, however, is only preliminary, and the real ritual act of arrest occurs in the presence of an inspector in the room of Fräulein Bürstner, where none of those present, not even K. himself, would have any right to be. K. is instructed to dress in formal clothes for the act. In Fräulein Bürstner's room there are, besides the inspector and the two warders, three young men whom K. does not recognize, or only later recognizes, clerks at the bank at which he holds a fairly high position. From the house opposite, strangers are watching. No reason is given for the arrest and, strangest of all, K. is allowed, in spite of the announcement of his arrest, to go to work at the bank and move about freely in other ways as well.

This freedom of movement after the arrest is the first thing that is reminiscent of Kafka's engagement in Berlin. At that time, he had the feeling that none of the events actually concerned him. He felt trapped and among virtual strangers. The relevant passage in his diary, already cited, reads: "Was tied hand and foot like a criminal. Had they sat me down in a corner bound in real chains, placed policemen in front of me and let me look on simply like that, it could not have been worse. And that was my engagement." The irksome aspect common to both procedures is their being public. The presence of both families at the engagement—he had always had a hard time keeping his own family at arm's length—drove him more and more back upon himself. Because of the pressure to which they were subjecting him, he felt that they were strangers. Among the guests there were members of the Bauer family whom he did not yet really know, as well as others, such as Grete Bloch's brother, who were strangers. Still others he might have seen fleetingly once or twice; but even Felice's mother, with whom he had already had a talk, always made him feel uneasy. As far as his own relatives were concerned, it was as if he had lost the ability to recognize them, because they were jointly performing a sort of act of violence against him.

A similar spectrum of strangers and acquaintances is present at Joseph K.'s arrest. There were the two warders and the inspector, entirely new figures; the people in the house opposite, whom he might have seen before, without their being of any concern to him; and the young men from his bank, whom he did see every day, but during the act of arrest, in which they participate simply by being present, they have become strangers to him.

Even more important is the place where the arrest occurs, Fräulein Bürstner's room. Her name begins with a B, like Bauer, but Grete Bloch's name also begins with a B. In the room there are family photos, and a white blouse is hanging from the window latch. At the time, no woman is present in the room, but the blouse is a conspicuous deputy.

Yet the intrusion into Fräulein Bürstner's room, with her not knowing of it, preoccupies K.; the thought of the disorder left there gives him no peace. When he comes home from the bank in the evening, he has a discussion with his landlady, Frau Grubach. In spite of the morning's events, she has not lost confidence in him. "It's a matter of your happiness," she says at the outset of one of her comforting statements.[14] The word for happiness here—*Glück*—is strangely disturbing, an interloper, reminding one of the letters to Felice, where *Glück* is always used ambiguously; in the letters the note it strikes could also, and primarily, mean *Unglück*—unhappiness, ill fortune. K. now remarks that he would like to apologize to Fräulein Bürstner, because he has made use of her room. Frau Grubach calms him down and shows him the room, where order has been restored: "And the blouse was no longer dangling from the latch of the window."[15] It is late in the evening and still Fräulein Bürstner has not come home. Frau Grubach indulges in various remarks about Fräulein Bürstner's private life, remarks that are somehow provocative. K. waits for her return, involves her, somewhat against her own will, in a conversation in her room about the morning's events, and while he is describing them he speaks in such a loud voice that someone in the next room gives a few sudden knocks. Fräulein Bürstner feels compromised and is unhappy about this; K., as if wanting to console her, kisses her forehead. He promises to tell the landlady that he will take all the blame, but she will hear nothing of it and urges K. into the entrance hall. K. then "seized her, and kissed her first on the lips, then all over the face, like some thirsty animal lapping greedily at a spring of long-sought fresh water. Finally he kissed her on the neck, right on the throat, and kept his lips there for a long time."[16] Returning to his room, he soon falls asleep, "but before doing so he thought for a little about his behavior, he was pleased with it, yet surprised that he was not still more pleased."[17]

It is difficult not to feel that Fräulein Bürstner in this scene stands for Grete Bloch. Kafka's longing for her is there, with strength and immediacy. The arrest, which derived from that tortured process of the engagement with Felice, has been transferred into the room of the other woman. K., who was aware of no guilt at all during the morning, becomes guilty through his conduct during the night, through his attack on Fräulein Bürstner. For "he was pleased with it."

The complex and almost insoluble situation in which Kafka found himself placed at the engagement is thus explicated by him with startling clarity in the first chapter of *The Trial*. He had very much wanted Grete Bloch to be present at the engagement, and had even shown an interest in what dress she would wear. It is not unthinkable that this dress has been transformed into the blouse that hung in Fräulein Bürstner's room. Despite his endeavors as the novel proceeds, K. does not manage to speak with Fräulein Bürstner about what has happened. She skillfully evades him, very much to his annoyance, and his nocturnal attack on her remains a secret, intact, shared by the two of them.

This, too, reminds one of Kafka's relationship with Grete Bloch. Whatever may have occurred between them has remained a secret. It cannot be supposed, since there is not a scrap of evidence for it, that this secret was divulged at the "tribunal" in the Askanische Hof. For there the question was his doubtful attitude to the engagement; the passages in his letters to Grete Bloch, which revealed this attitude, concerned Felice and the engagement. The actual secret between Grete and Kafka was not touched on by either of them. Nothing in the correspondence sheds any light on this matter: obviously Grete destroyed some of the letters.

To understand now how the "tribunal," which had an enormous impact on Kafka, became the execution in the last chapter of *The Trial*, we must additionally consider several passages from the diaries and from letters. Toward the end of July, he sets out to describe the sequence of events,

Elias Canetti

hurriedly and provisionally, as it were from an external standpoint:

"The tribunal in the hotel. . . . F.'s face. She patted her hair with her hand, . . . yawned. Suddenly she gathered herself together and said very studied, hostile things she had long been saving up. The trip back with Miss Bl. . . . At her parents'. Her mother's occasional tears. I recited my lesson. Her father understood the thing from every side. . . . They agreed that I was right, there was nothing, or not much, that could be said against me. Devilish in my innocence. Miss Bl.'s apparent guilt. . . .

"Why did her parents and aunt wave after me?[18]

"The next day didn't visit her parents again. Merely sent a messenger with a letter of farewell. Letter dishonest and coquettish. 'Don't think badly of me.' Speech from the gallows."[19]

Thus, already by July 27, two weeks after the events, the "place of execution" has fixed itself in his mind. With the word Gerichtshof ("tribunal"), he had entered the sphere of the novel. With Richtplatz ("gallows," or "place of execution"), its goal and end are foreshadowed. This early fixing of the goal is worth noting. It explains the sure development of The Trial.

One person in Berlin was "unimaginably kind" to him (441), and he never forgot it: Erna, Felice's sister. There is the following statement about her in the diaries: "I think of the walk we, E. and I, took from the trolley to the Lehrter railroad station. Neither of us spoke, I thought nothing but that each step taken was that much of a gain for me. And E. is nice to me, believes in me for some incomprehensible reason, in spite of having seen me before the tribunal; now and then I even feel the effect of this faith in me, without, however, fully believing in the feeling."[20]

Erna's kindness and the enigmatic waving of the parents' hands, after it was all over, coalesce on the penultimate page of *The Trial*, just before the execution, in that surpassingly marvelous and unforgettable passage: "His glance fell on the top story of the house adjoining the quarry. With a flicker as of a light going up, the casements of a window there suddenly flew open; a human figure, faint and insubstantial at that distance and that height, leaned abruptly far forward and stretched both arms still farther. Who was it? A friend? A good man? Someone who sympathized? Someone who wanted to help? Was it one person only? Or was it mankind? Was help at hand?"[21]

(In the original version there appeared, a few sentences further on, the questions: "Where was the Judge? Where the High Court of Justice? I have something to say. I lift up my hands.")[22]

At the Askanische Hof Kafka did not defend himself. He said nothing. He refused to acknowledge the court presiding over him and expressed this refusal by silence. This silence lasted a long time: for three months there was no communication between him and Felice. But he sometimes wrote to her sister Erna, who believed in him. In October, Grete Bloch recalled her role as mediator and tried to resume relations. Her letter to him has not been preserved, but his answer has: "You do say that I hate you; but this isn't true. . . . It's true that at the Askanische Hof you sat in judgment over me—it was horrible for you, for me, for everyone—but it only appeared to be so; in fact I was sitting in your place, which to this day I have not left" (436).

One might easily read the end of this remark as a self-accusation, a self-accusation that began long before and goes on forever. But I do not think that this completely explains it. Much more important, it seems to me, is Kafka's removing Grete Bloch here from her seat of judgment: he thrusts her away and sets himself up in the place she had presumed to occupy. There is no external tribunal that he acknowledges; he is his own tribunal, but very much so, and that tribunal will always be in session. As for her usurpation, he says nothing stronger than "it only appeared to be so"; but his seeing through her presumption makes it look as if she had never really sat in judgment. Instead of excluding her by force, he shows that she was an illusion. He refuses to fight with her, but the noblesse of his reply barely conceals how little he concedes to her, not even the hatred of conflict. He is cognizant of the fact that he is conducting his trial against himself; nobody else is fit to conduct it; and when he wrote this letter he was far from bringing it to a conclusion.

Two weeks later, in his first, very long letter to Felice, he writes that his silence at the Askanische Hof was not due to defiance, not a very convincing assertion. For in the very next sentence he writes: "What you said was so clear I have no wish to repeat it; but it included certain things that ought to be almost impossible for one person to say to another. . . . I no longer object to your having brought along Frl. Bl[och]; after all, I had almost discredited you in that letter to her; she had a right to be present. But that you should have allowed your sister [Erna], whom I hardly knew at the time, to come along as well—that I could not understand" (437).

The outcome of the matter, the breaking of the engagement, was as he had wished; on that count he could only feel relief. But what hurt him, what most deeply shamed him, was the public nature of the proceedings. The shame at this humiliation, the gravity of which can only be rightly measured against his pride, remained with him, concentrated: its fruit was *The Trial*, and it flowed undiminished into the last chapter. K. allows himself to be led to his execution in silence, almost without resisting. That resistance of his, which with its tenacity constitutes the movement of the novel, is something he gives up, suddenly and completely. His walk through the city is like a synthesis of all his other walks that were connected with his resistance: "And then before them Fräulein Bürstner appeared, mounting a small flight of steps leading into the square from a low-lying side-street. It was not quite certain that it was she, but the resemblance was close enough."[23] He starts to walk, and now it is he who chooses the direction: "They suffered him now to lead the way, and he followed the direction taken by the girl ahead of him, not that he wanted to overtake her or to keep her in sight as long as possible, but only that he might not forget the lesson she had brought into his mind."[24] It is the lesson *(Mahnung)* that reminds him of his secret and of the unspoken guilt. It is independent of the court, which has withdrawn from him; independent of the accusation, about which he never could find out anything. Nevertheless, it strengthens him in his task of giving up resistance on his last walk. The shame, however, of which mention has been made above, has a longer reach, right into the last sentences of all: "But the hands of one of the partners were already at K.'s throat, while the other thrust the knife deep into his heart and turned it there twice. With failing eyes K. could still see the two of them immediately before him, cheek leaning against cheek, watching the final act. 'Like a dog!' he said; it was as if the shame of it must outlive him."[25]

The last humiliation is the public character of this death, a death that is observed by the two executioners, their faces close to his face, their own cheeks leaning together. K.'s "failing eyes" bear witness to his death's public character. His last thought is of the shame that may be strong enough to outlive him, and the last words he speaks are "Like a dog!"

In August 1914, as already mentioned, Kafka began to write. He managed to devote himself to his work every day for three months, with only two evenings away from it, as he remarks with some pride in a later letter. Mainly he was writing *The Trial*, the real object of his impetus. But there were also other writings; uninterrupted work on the novel was evidently not possible. In August he also began his "Memoirs of the Kalda Railroad," never completed. In October he took two weeks' vacation, with a view to getting on with the novel, but instead he wrote during this time "In the Penal Colony" and the last chapter of *Amerika*.

Already during this vacation the two women tried to re-establish contact with him. First he receives a letter from Grete Bloch; a passage from his reply was quoted above. This reply "sounds unyielding"—he copies it into his diary and comments: "I know it is certain that I shall live on alone."[26] He considers his aversion to Felice "at the sight of her dancing with her severe eyes lowered, or when she ran her hand over her nose and hair in the Askanische Hof shortly before she left, and the numberless moments of complete estrangement."[27] But he has nevertheless been "playing" with the letter all through the evening; his work has come to a standstill, although he feels capable of writing.

"It would be best for all of us if she would not answer, but she will answer and I shall wait for her answer."[28]

By the very next day his feelings both of defensiveness and of enticement have come to a pitch. He has been living quietly, without any real connection with Felice, has dreamed about her as if she were a dead person who could never come to life again, "and now, when I am offered a chance to come near her, she is at once the center of every-thing again. She is probably also interfering with my work. How very much a stranger she has sometimes seemed to me these latter days when I would think of her, of all the people I had ever met the most remote."[29]

The "center of everything"—that is the real danger for him. She must not be allowed to become such a center; this is why he cannot marry, either her or anybody else. The home she is always wanting, that is she herself, the center. He can only be his own forever-vulnerable center. The vulnerabili-ty of his body and of his brain is the real precondition for his writing. Often as it may seem as if he is anxious to find protection, security against this vulnerability, all these ex-ertions are deceptive: he needs his solitude, in the form of *exposure*.

Ten days later a reply comes from Grete Bloch. "I am completely undecided as to how to answer it. Thoughts so base that I cannot even write them down."[30]

What he calls base thoughts coalesce to form a shield whose efficacy should not this time be underestimated. At the end of October he writes a very long letter to Felice, announcing its arrival in advance by telegram. It is a letter that shows amazing detachment. There is hardly a single complaint in it; it is perceptibly, for Kafka, a healthy and aggressive letter.

He had not thought, of course, that he would write to

her—at the Askanische Hof it had become only too evident
that letters were worthless, as was anything in writing. Much
more calmly than in earlier letters, he explains to her that it
was his work that had to be defended against her, with all his
might. He describes his present life, with which he seems not
unsatisfied. He is living alone in his oldest sister's apartment
(his brother-in-law is away at the war, so she is living with
the parents). He writes that he is alone in these three rooms,
meeting nobody, not even his friends. For the last three
months he has worked every day at his writing. This is only
the second evening he has not done so. He is not happy, to be
sure, but sometimes he is satisfied that he is doing his duty,
as far as present circumstances permit.

It is this kind of life that he has always striven for, he says;
but such a conception of life always made her dislike him.
He enumerates for her all the occasions on which she
showed this dislike, the last and decisive one being her
outburst at the Askanische Hof. It was his duty to watch over
his work, and her dislike was the greatest danger to it.

As a concrete example of the difficulties between them,
he cites in a detailed way their disagreement about an
apartment: "What you wanted was perfectly reasonable: a
pleasant, pleasantly furnished, family apartment, such as is
inhabited by all families of both your and my social standing. . . . But your whole idea about the apartment, what does
it show? It shows that you agree with the others, not with me.
. . . These others, when they get married, are very nearly
satiated, and marriage to them is but the final, great, deli-
cious mouthful. Not so for me, I am not satiated, I haven't
started a business that's expected to expand from one year of
marriage to another; I don't need a permanent home from
whose bourgeois orderliness I propose to run this business—not only do I not need this kind of home, it actually

frightens me. I am so hungry for my work . . . ; here, however, the conditions are antagonistic to my work, so if I set up house according to your wishes under these conditions, it would mean . . . that I am attempting to make these conditions permanent, which is the worst thing that can befall me" (440).

At the end of the letter he defends his writing to her sister, saying that he will write to Erna the next day.

Among the diary entries for November 1, there is a remark that is most unusual: "Much self-satisfaction all day."[31] This self-satisfaction must relate to the long letter, which he had most probably mailed by now. He had resumed relations with Felice, but had not yielded any ground. His position was now clear and hard, and although he sometimes expressed doubts about it, it remained so for a long time to come. On November 3 he writes in his diary: "Since August, the fourth day on which I have written nothing. The letters are the cause of it; I'll try to write none at all or only very short ones."[32]

So now it is his own letters that are disturbing his work. This is very important and illuminating. As long as he is still busy dissociating the "trial" from Felice, he can hardly turn toward her again with such detailed attentiveness as in the October letter. That would inevitably confuse the novel; every time he scrutinizes their relationship, he is taken back into the time that preceded his writing of the novel. It is as if such backward looks threaten to erode its roots. Thus, from now on he avoids writing to her; not a single letter has been preserved from the next three-month period, until the end of January 1915. He tries with all his might to keep his grip on his work; he cannot always do so, but he does not give up trying. At the beginning of December he reads "In the Penal Colony" to his friends, and is "not entirely dissatisfied." The outcome of the same day is the remark: "I'll go on working regardless of everything, it must be possible in spite of the office or the lack of sleep."[33]

On December 5 he receives from Erna a letter about the Bauer family situation, which has become much worse since the death of the father a few weeks before. Kafka regards himself as the ruin of the family, without feeling in any way emotionally attached to it. "Only ruin has effect. I have made F. unhappy, weakened the resistance of all those who need her so much now, contributed to the death of her father, come between F. and E., and in the end made E. unhappy too. . . . I am indeed sufficiently punished in general, even my attitude toward the family is punishment enough; I have also suffered so much that I shall never recover from it . . . ; for the moment, however, my relationship to them causes me little suffering, at least less than F. or E."[34]

The effect of this embracing guilt that he ascribed to himself—as the ruin of the entire Bauer family—was, as might be expected, a calming one. There was no place in it for the particulars of his behavior toward Felice; the larger context of general family ruin absorbed all particulars. For six full weeks, until January 17, neither Felice nor Erna nor any other member of the unfortunate family is mentioned in the diaries or letters. In December, he writes the "In the Cathedral" chapter of *The Trial*, and begins two other pieces, "The Village Schoolmaster" ["The Giant Mole"] and "The Assistant Attorney." He draws up the balance of the year's work in his diary entry of December 31; this is quite contrary to his custom, more like something in the diaries of Hebbel: "Have been working since August, in general not little and not badly."[35] Then, after a few of his inevitable qualifications and self-admonitions, there follows a list of the six

works that had been preoccupying him. Without a knowledge of the manuscripts, to which I have no access, it is
difficult to tell how much of *The Trial* was on paper at this
time. Certainly a very large part of it had been written. In any
case, it is an impressive list, and one has no hesitation in
calling these latter five months of 1914 the second great
period in Kafka's life as a writer.

On January 23 and 24, 1915, Kafka and Felice met at
Bodenbach on the frontier. Only six days prior to the meeting there is a note about the plan in the diaries: "Saturday I
shall see F. If she loves me, I do not deserve it. . . . I have been
very self-satisfied of late and knew a variety of arguments by
which to defend and assert myself against F."[36] Three days
later he writes: "The end of writing. When will it catch up
again? In what a bad state I am going to meet F.! . . . My
inability to prepare for the meeting; whereas last week I
could hardly shake off all the ideas it aroused in me."[37]

It was his first meeting with Felice since the "tribunal,"
and she could hardly have made a more irksome impression
on him. *The Trial* had become dissociated from her, so he
could view her with greater detachment and freedom.
Nonetheless, the marks left on him by the "tribunal" turned
out to be permanent. In a letter he noted his impression of
her with restraint, but in his diaries he did so without
forbearance:

"Each of us silently says to himself that the other is
immovable and merciless. I yield not a particle of my de-
mand for a fantastic life arranged solely in the interest of my
work; she, indifferent to every mute request, wants the
average: a comfortable home, an interest on my part in the
factory, good food, bed at eleven, central heating; sets my
watch—which for the past three months has been an hour

and a half fast—right to the minute. . . . We were alone two hours in the room. Round about, me only boredom and despair. We haven't yet had a single good moment together during which I could have breathed freely. . . . I also read aloud to her, the sentences proceeded in a disgusting confusion, with no relationship to the listener, who lay on the sofa with closed eyes and silently received them. . . . What I said was true and was acknowledged to be true: each loves the other person as he is. But doesn't think it possible to live with him as he is."[38]

Her intrusiveness is most painful when it concerns his watch. That his watch is set differently from other people's means for him a tiny piece of freedom. She puts it right, to the actual minute, a thoughtless act which sabotages this freedom, an accommodation to her time, the time of the office, the factory. The word "loves," however, in the penultimate sentence, sounds like a slap in the face; it could just as well be "hates."

From now on, the character of the correspondence changes completely. Kafka will never again relapse into his old way of writing to Felice. He guards against involving her again in the "trial"; what is left of it hardly pertains to her. He resolves to write to her every fortnight, and does not even keep this resolve. Of all the letters, eighty per cent come from the first two years, up to the end of 1914; the letters of the three years 1915–17 occupy no more than twenty per cent of the book. A few letters from the later period have been lost, to be sure; but, even if they had not been, the proportions would be essentially the same. Everything he writes to her now becomes much more infrequent and also shorter; he begins to use postcards—the correspondence of 1916 consists largely of these. A practical reason for their use was that postcards passed more easily the censorship of mails between Austria and Germany during the war. The tone has changed: often now it is Felice who complains about his not writing; she is now always the wooer, he on the defensive. In 1915, two years after publication, she even— miracle of miracles—reads *Meditation*.

The meeting in Bodenbach can be regarded as a watershed in the relations between Kafka and Felice. As soon as he had come to view her as pitilessly as he viewed himself, he ceased to be so helplessly embroiled in his conception of her. After the "tribunal" he had put aside all thoughts of her, knowing full well that a letter from her might bring them out again into the open. But as a result of the courage that he mustered for the new confrontation with her, a new balance of power entered the relationship. One is inclined to call the new period one of *rectification:* he, who once drew strength from her efficiency, now tries to make a different person of her.

Is the story of a five-year-long withdrawal so important, one may ask, that it has to be considered in such detail? Interest in a writer can certainly be carried to great lengths. And if the documents are as copious as they are in this case, then it can become irresistibly tempting to know them all and to grasp their internal coherence; the wealth of the documentation only sharpens the critic's appetite. Man considers himself the measure of all things, but he is still almost unknown. His progress in self-knowledge is minimal; every new theory obscures more of him than it illuminates. Only unimpeded concrete inquiry into particular human beings makes gradual advance possible. Since this has long been the case, and the best minds have always been aware of it, a human being who offers himself to knowledge so completely is, under any circumstances, an incomparable stroke of luck. But, in Kafka's case, there is even more to it, as anyone can feel who comes close to him in his private sphere. There is something most profoundly exciting about this tenacious attempt, on the part of a man who was lacking in power, to withdraw from power in whatever form it might appear. Before describing the further course of his relationship with Felice, it would seem appropriate to show how filled his mind was with the very phenomenon that has become most pressing and terrible, above all others, in our epoch. Of all writers, Kafka is the greatest expert on power. He experienced it in all its aspects, and he gave shape to this experience.

One of his central themes is humiliation; it is also the theme that can be most easily observed. As early as "The Judgment"—for Kafka the first work of his that counts—the theme can be grasped without difficulty. There it is a question of two degradations which are interdependent, that of the father and that of the son. The father feels endangered by the supposed intrigues of the son. During his accusatory speech he stands up on the bed, and thus, much taller in relation to the son, he attempts to convert his own degradation into its opposite, the humiliation of the son: he condemns him to death by drowning. The son does not acknowledge the legitimacy of the judgment, but he carries it out and thus concedes the measure of humiliation that costs him his life. The humiliation is strictly framed in its own terms; absurd as it is, the effect it makes constitutes the story's strength.

In *The Metamorphosis*, degradation is concentrated in the body that suffers it: the degraded object is, from the first moment, compactly there. Instead of a son, who feeds and supports the family, all of a sudden there is an insect. This transformation exposes him, inescapably, to humiliation; an entire family feels provoked to inflict it actively. Hesitantly the humiliation begins. Time is allowed for its expansion and intensification. Gradually all the characters, almost helplessly and against their will, participate in it. They recapitulate the act that is given at the outset: it is the family itself that transforms Gregor Samsa, irretrievably, into an insect. What was an insect becomes, in the social context, vermin.

The novel *Amerika* is full of humiliations, but they are not of this unheard-of or irreparable kind. They are contained within the conception of the continent whose name becomes the book's title. Rossmann's first being raised up by his uncle and then his sudden fall can serve as an example of much else in the story. The harshness of life in the new country is compensated for by its greater social mobility. The person humiliated is always filled with lively expectation; every fall can be followed by a miracle which raises a person up again. Nothing that happens to Rossmann has the fatality of something final. Thus this book is the most hopeful and the least troubling of Kafka's narratives.

In *The Trial*, degradation issues from a superior source which is much more complex than the family in *The Metamorphosis*. The court, once it has made itself noticeable, degrades by retreating: it veils itself in a secrecy which no effort can unravel. The tenacity of efforts to do so only proves how senseless the attempt is. Every clue that is followed up seems to be irrelevant. The question as to guilt or innocence, which is the only possible reason for the court's existence, remains a nonessential one; it even turns out that guilt originates only in ceaseless endeavor to find out about the court. The basic theme of humiliation, however, and of its occurrence in human relationships, is varied through the separate episodes. The scene with the painter Titorelli, which begins with the bewildering mockery of the small girls, concludes, as K. thinks he is about to suffocate in the tiny studio, with the inspection and purchase of paintings that are all alike. K. also has to witness the humiliation of others: he sees the tradesman Block kneeling by the lawyer's bedside and changing into a sort of dog; even that, like everything else, is ultimately to no avail. (We have already considered the conclusion of *The Trial*, the "shame" of the public execution.)

The image of the dog, with this meaning assigned to it, keeps appearing in Kafka's writings and in letters where he refers to events in his life. Thus he writes to Felice concerning the incident in the spring of 1914: "when running along behind you in the Tiergarten, you always on the point of vanishing altogether, and I on the point of prostrating myself; only when thus humiliated, more deeply than any dog, am I able to do it" (372). At the end of the first paragraph of "In the Penal Colony," the image of the condemned man in his chains is epitomized in the following sentence: "In any case, the condemned man looked so like a submissive dog that one might have thought he could be left to run free on the surrounding hills and would only need to be whistled for when the execution was due to begin."[39]

The Castle, which belongs to a much later period of Kafka's life, introduces a new dimension of spaciousness into his work. An impression of spaciousness is conveyed here less by the presence of a landscape than by the more complete, more richly populated world that the novel presents. Here, too, as in *The Trial*, power is evasive, it withdraws: Klamm, the hierarchy of officials, the castle. You can see them, but cannot be certain you have seen them; the real relationship between the powerless human beings who live at the foot of the castle hill and the officials is one of waiting for superiors. The question of the *raison d'être* of the superiors is never asked. But what issues from above and spreads among the ordinary people is humiliation at the hands of the superiors. The only act of resistance to this superior power, Amalia's refusal to do the will of an official, ends with the whole family's being ostracized from the village community. The writer's fascination concerns the inferiors who wait in vain; the superior power, presiding over the welter of its files—that is his aversion. The religious element that many claim to find in *The Castle* may be there, but it is *naked*, an insatiable and incomprehensible longing for what is above. No author ever wrote a clearer attack on subjection to the superior, whether one views the latter as a higher power or as a merely terrestrial one. For all sovereignty has here become one, and is shown to be abominable. Belief and power coalesce; both produce dubious effects. The submissiveness of those who are sacrificed, to whom it never occurs even to dream of an alternative way of life, would make a very rebel out of a person whom the palaver of ideologies—not a few of which have failed—never even remotely touched.

From the beginning, Kafka sided with the humiliated. Many people have done this, and, in order to accomplish something, they have associated with others. The sense of strength thus obtained soon took away their acute feeling of humiliation, of which there is no end—humiliation does continue, day by day and hour by hour. Kafka kept each such experience apart from similar ones, but also apart from those of other men. It was not given him to shed his experiences by sharing or communicating them; he preserved them, with a kind of obduracy, as if they were his most significant possession. One might say that this obduracy was the real thing that was given him.

People as sensitive as Kafka are perhaps not so rare; more rare is the peculiarly slow development of all his reactions. He often speaks of his bad memory, but in reality nothing escapes him. The acuteness of his memory is reflected in the way he corrects and completes Felice's imprecise memories of earlier years. It is a fact, all the same, that he cannot always freely recall his memories. His obduracy keeps them out of his reach; he cannot, like other writers, play with his memories irresponsibly. This obduracy follows its own stringent laws—one might say that it helps him to husband his defensive forces. It enables him not to obey commands immediately, yet to feel their sting as if he had obeyed, and then to use the sting to strengthen his resistance. Yet when he does eventually obey, the commands are no longer the same, for by then he has taken them out of their temporal context, considered them from every angle, weakened them by reflection, and thus stripped them of their dangerous character.

This procedure would require more precise consideration, to be verified by concrete examples. I shall offer only one example: Kafka's obstinate resistance to certain foods. He lives for a long time with his family, but makes no concessions to their prevailing eating habits, which he treats as commands to be warded off. Thus he sits at his parents' table in a food-world of his own making, which earns him his father's deepest dislike. But his way of warding off commands here gives him strength for similar practices in other situations, and also with regard to other persons. During his struggle against Felice's fatal ideas about marriage, a cardinal role is played by his emphasis on these traits. Blow for blow, he defends his position against the conformity she expects from him. But hardly has the engagement been broken off than he allows himself even meat. In a letter to his Prague friends, from the Baltic coast resort where he had gone to stay soon after the Berlin "tribunal," he describes, not without distaste, his meat-eating excesses. Even months later, he tells Felice with satisfaction how he went with her sister Erna to eat meat shortly after the breaking of the engagement. If Felice had been present, he writes, he would have ordered *Krachmandel*. [40] Thus, once he is no longer under any pressure from Felice, he carries out commands that no longer signify subjection.

Kafka's taciturnity, his secretiveness even where friends were concerned, must be regarded as exercises in obduracy. He does not always realize what he is keeping silent about. But when his characters, in *The Trial* or especially in *The Castle*, make their frequently voluble speeches, one senses that his own floodgates are being opened: he discovers language. Seldom does his obduracy allow him to speak, but here, in the apparent disguise of a character, it suddenly bestows upon him the freedom of speech. These are not like the confessions of characters in Dostoevski—there is a different temperature, much less heated. Moreover, nothing here is amorphous; rather it is the fluent playing of a clearly defined instrument, which is capable of certain sounds only—the fluency of a fastidious but unmistakable virtuoso.

The history of his resistance to his father, not to be approached in the usual banal terms, is also the early history of his obduracy. Much of what has been said about this relationship seems to be altogether wrong; Kafka's sovereign perspective on psychoanalysis ought to have helped critics to detach from its constricting domain his own person at least. His struggle with his father was essentially never anything but a struggle against superior power as such. He hated his family as a whole; his father was simply the most powerful part of this family. When the danger arose of his having a family of his own, his struggle with Felice had the same motive and the same character.

It is worth while to recall once again Kafka's silence at the Askanische Hof, the most revealing instance of his obduracy. He does not react, as any other person would have done; he does not retaliate with counteraccusations. Considering how sensitive he was, it can hardly be doubted that he takes in and feels everything said against him. And what is said to him is not "repressed"—a term that might otherwise have some relevance. What he did was preserve it, remaining well aware of it; often he thinks about it, it presses so often upon his mind that the process should be regarded as the antithesis of repression. What is blocked is any external reaction that might betray the internal effect. Whatever he preserves in this way is sharp as a knife; but neither ill will nor hatred, neither anger nor resentment can ever compel him to abuse the knife. It stays aloof from emotion, an autonomous structure. But insofar as it keeps out of emotion's reach, it withdraws Kafka from the sphere of power.

Here some apology might be due for the naïve use of the word "power." Yet Kafka himself uses it unhesitatingly, in spite of all its ambiguities. The word appears throughout his writings in the most varied contexts. Due to his shunning "big" words, overcharged words, there is not a single "rhetorical" work by him. Accordingly, he will never become less readable; the continuous emptying and refilling of

words, a process that induces aging in practically all literature, can never affect him. But he never shuns the words
"Macht" ("power") and *"mächtig"* ("powerful"); both are
among his unavoided, unavoidable words. It would certainly be worth the trouble to trace all the passages where
they appear in his writings, diaries, and letters.

It is not, however, only the word, it is also the thing, in all
its infinite complexity, that he articulates with unrivaled
courage and clarity. For, since he fears power in any form,
since the real aim of his life is to withdraw from it, in
whatever form it may appear, he detects it, identifies it,
names it, and creates figures of it in every instance where
others would accept it as being nothing out of the ordinary.

In a note to be found in the volume *Dearest Father,* he
renders the animal nature of power, a stupendous cosmic
image in eight lines: "I was defenseless confronted with the
figure, calmly it sat there at the table, gazing at the table-top.
I walked round it in circles, feeling myself throttled by it.
And around me there walked a third, feeling throttled by
me. Around that third there walked a fourth, feeling throttled by him. And so it went on, right out to the circling of the
constellations, and further still. Everything felt the grip at the
throat."[41]

The threat, the throttling, spreads from the inmost center,
where it originates, a gravitational force of strangulation,
which sustains each concentric circle "right out to the circling of the constellations, and further still." The Pythago-
rean harmony of the spheres has become a sphere-system of
violence, with human gravity predominating, each individual representing a separate sphere.

He feels the threat of teeth, so intensely that it is the
separate teeth, rather than their rows, which have him in
their grip: "It was an ordinary day; it bared its teeth at me; I

too was held by teeth and could not wriggle out of their grip; I did not know how they were holding me, for they were not clenched; nor did I see them in the form of the two rows of a set of teeth, but merely some here and some there. I wanted to hold on to them and vault over them, but I did not succeed in doing so."[42]

In a letter to Felice he coins the appalling phrase "the terror of standing upright." He interprets a dream of hers that she has told him; the interpretation is such that one can gather the content without much difficulty: "Had you not been lying on the ground among the animals, you would have been unable to see the sky and the stars and wouldn't have been set free. Perhaps you wouldn't have survived the terror of standing upright. I feel much the same; it is a mutual dream that you have dreamed for us both" (447). One must lie down with the beasts in order to be set free, or redeemed (erlöst). Standing upright signifies the power of man over beast; but precisely in this most obvious attitude man is exposed, visible, vulnerable. For this power is also guilt, and only on the ground, lying among the animals, can one see the stars, which free one from this terrifying power of man.

The loudest passage in Kafka's work tells of this guilt of man with regard to the animals. The following paragraph appears in "An Old Manuscript," from A Country Doctor:

"Not long ago the butcher thought he might at least spare himself the trouble of slaughtering, and so one morning he brought along a live ox. But he will never dare to do that again. I lay for a whole hour flat on the floor at the back of my workshop with my head muffled in all the clothes and rugs and pillows I had simply to keep from hearing the bellowing of that ox, which the nomads were leaping on from all sides, tearing morsels out of its living flesh with their teeth. It had been quiet for a long time before I risked coming out; they were lying overcome around the remains of the carcass like drunkards around a wine cask."[43]

"It had been quiet for a long time . . ." Might one say that the narrator was withdrawing from what could not be endured, that he has found peace again? Or, after such bellowing, can there be no peace? It is Kafka's own position; but all the clothes, rugs, and pillows in the world could not lastingly silence the bellowing in his ears. If he ever withdrew from it, it was only to hear it again, for the bellowing did not stop. To be sure, the word "withdraw" here is a very imprecise one to apply to Kafka. In his case it means that he sought tranquility, silence, so as to hear only the bellowing—which was nothing less than fear.

Confronted as he was with power on all sides, his obduracy sometimes offered him a reprieve. But if it was insufficient, or if it failed him, he trained himself to disappear; here the helpful aspect of his physical thinness is revealed, though often, as we know, he despised it. By means of physical diminution, he withdrew power *from himself*, and thus had less part in it; this asceticism, too, was directed against power. The same penchant for disappearing reveals itself in his relation to his own name. In two of his novels, *The Trial* and *The Castle*, he reduces his name to the initial K. In the letters to Felice, his name becomes shorter and shorter and finally disappears altogether.

Most astounding of all is another method he practices, with a sovereign skill matched only by the Chinese: transformation into something small. Since he abominated violence, but did not credit himself with the strength to combat it, he enlarged the distance between the stronger entity and himself by becoming smaller and smaller in relation to it. Through this shrinkage he gained two advantages: he evaded the threat by becoming too diminutive for it, and he freed himself from all exceptionable means of violence; the small animals into which he liked to transform himself were harmless ones.

An early letter to Max Brod sheds a very clear light on the genesis of this unusual aptitude. It comes from the year 1904, when Kafka was twenty-one years old; I call it the Mole Letter and quote from it as much as seems necessary for an understanding of Kafka's transformation into something small. Before doing so, I shall quote, by way of preface, a statement from a letter written during the previous year to a school friend, Oskar Pollak: "One should honor the mole and his kind but not make him into one's patron saint." That is no great dictum; nevertheless the mole enters the picture here for the first time. Already a special note sounds in the phrase "his kind"; and one should not fail to remark that the warning against making a saint of the mole adumbrates its later significance. Here is the passage from the letter to Max Brod: "We burrow through ourselves like moles and emerge out of our vaults of sand all blackened and velvet-haired, with our poor little red feet outstretched for tender sympathy.

"While I was out on a walk my dog came upon a mole that was trying to cross the road. He kept leaping at him and wouldn't leave him alone, for he is a young dog, and timid. At first I was amused and liked especially the mole's excitement as he looked for a hole in the hard surface of the road, altogether desperately and ineffectually. But then suddenly, when the dog struck him once more with an outstretched paw, he shrieked Ks, kss, just like that. And then I thought—no, I did not think anything. I was simply in a state of delusion, because on that day my head was hanging so heavily that in the evening I noticed with amazement that my chin had grown into my chest."[44]

The dog, let us note, the dog hunting the mole, was Kafka's dog; he was its master. For the mole—who, scared to death, looks for a hole in the hard road, a hole in which to hide—he himself does not exist; the animal is afraid only of the dog, its senses are open only for the latter. But he, Kafka, so exalted above them, by his upright stance, his height, and his ownership of the dog, which could never threaten him, simply laughs at the desperate and ineffectual movements of the mole. The mole does not realize that it could turn to him for help; it has not learned to pray, and it is capable of nothing but its small screams. They are the only sounds that touch the god, for here he is the god, the supreme being, the zenith of power, and in this case God is even present. The mole screams *Ks, kss,* and the onlooker, hearing this scream, transforms himself into the mole. Without having to fear his dog, which is his slave, he feels what it is to be a mole.

The unexpected scream is not the only vehicle for transformation into something small. Another is the "poor little red feet," raised like hands that beg for compassion. In the fragment "Memoirs of the Kalda Railroad," dated August 1914, there is a related attempt to approach a dying rat through the medium of its little "hands":

"As for the rats that sometimes attacked my provisions, my long knife sufficed to deal with them. During the first days, when I was still eagerly taking in everything, I spitted one of these rats on the point of my knife and held it before me at eye level against the wall. You can see small animals clearly only if you hold them before you at eye level; if you stoop down to them on the ground and look at them there, you acquire a false, imperfect notion of them. The most striking feature of these rats was their claws—large, somewhat hollow, and yet pointed at the ends, they were well suited to dig with. Hanging against the wall in front of me in its final agony, it rigidly stretched out its claws in what seemed to be an unnatural way; they were like small hands reaching out to you."[45]

One must view small animals at eye level to see them accurately. This is tantamount to raising them to equal status. Stooping to the earth—a sort of condescension—gives one a false, incomplete conception of them. This raising of smaller animals to eye level makes one think of Kafka's tendency to magnify such creatures: the insect in *The Metamorphosis*, the molelike creature in "The Burrow." Through the closer approach to the animal and the animal's resultant magnification, transformation into something small becomes a more plastic, tangible, credible process.

An interest comparable to Kafka's in very small animals, especially insects, is to be found elsewhere only in the life and literature of the Chinese. From very early times, the Chinese numbered among their favorite animals the cricket. During the Sung Dynasty it became customary for people to keep crickets that were trained and provoked to fight one another. People kept them, for example, in walnut shells inside their shirts; the shells were furnished to provide for the crickets' needs. The owner of a famous cricket would feed flies with blood from his own arm, and when the flies were gorged he would chop them up and offer this hash to the cricket, in order to rouse its lust for battle. Special brushes and techniques were invented for provoking the combatants; and then, squatting or lying on their stomachs, people would watch the crickets fight. A little creature that had distinguished itself by unusual courage would be honored with the name of a general from Chinese history, people supposing that this general's soul had now taken up residence in the cricket's body. Thanks to Buddhism, most people regarded belief in the transmigration of souls as something altogether natural, so such a notion was nothing abstruse. The search for suitable crickets for the imperial court covered the entire land, and very high prices were paid for promising specimens. The story is told that, during the time the Sung empire was being overrun by the Mongols, the Chinese commander-in-chief was lying flat on his stomach watching a cricket fight when he received the news that the capital was surrounded by the enemy and in the greatest danger. He was incapable of separating himself from the crickets; first he had to see who was the winner here. The capital fell, and that was the end of the Sung empire.

Even much earlier, during the Tang period, crickets were kept in little cages on account of their chirping. But whether people held them up to observe them more closely and attentively while they chirped, or, because they were valuable, always carried them under their shirts and then took them out in order to tend their dwellings with care—either way people must have lifted them up to eye level, as Kafka recommended. People saw them on a basis of equality, and when the crickets were supposed to fight, people crouched down or lay on the ground. The crickets' souls were still those of renowned commanders, and the outcome of their battles could seem more important than the fate of a great empire.

There are many Chinese stories in which small animals play a role; especially frequent are stories in which crickets, ants, and bees accept a human being into their company, and behave toward him as human beings might. Kafka's letters do not make it clear whether or not he read the book *Chinese Ghost and Love Stories,* edited by Martin Buber, in which several stories of the kind appear. (He does mention this book in laudatory terms; and to his chagrin—this is during the time of his jealousy toward other writers—it.

turns out that Felice has bought a copy for herself.) But in any case, by virtue of some of his stories, Kafka belongs in the annals of Chinese literature. Often since the eighteenth century, European authors have taken up Chinese themes. But the only writer of the Western world who is essentially Chinese is Kafka.* In an observation that might almost come from a Taoist text, he has epitomized what "small-ness" meant for him: "Two possibilities: making oneself infinitely small or being so. The second is perfection, that is to say, inactivity, the first is beginning, that is to say, action."[46]

I realize that I have only touched here on a small part of what might be said about power and transformation in Kafka. A larger book would be called for if one were to undertake a complete or detailed treatment; here the story of his relationship with Felice, with three years of it still to come, must be followed to its end.

Of all the lean years of this relationship, 1915 was the leanest. Its symbol was Bodenbach: once Kafka had spoken or written something, its effect held for a long time. First of all, as a result of the confrontation, Felice did receive a few

---

* In support of this view, I would like to mention that Arthur Waley, whose connoisseurship in the field of Chinese literature was unrivaled, shared my opinion and discussed it in detail on many occasions. Kafka was certainly for this very reason the one German prose writer whom Waley read with passionate attention; he was as familiar with his work as with that of Po Chu-i and the Buddhist novel *Monkey*, both of which he had translated. During our conversations, there was often talk of Kafka's "natural" Taoism, but, duly respecting all the Chinese aspects of his work, we also discussed his special kind of ritualism. For Waley, the best instances were "The Refusal" and "The Great Wall of China"; other works were also mentioned.

further letters, but they became less and less frequent. In these, Kafka complained about his inability to write anything—now he really had come to the end of his resources again—and about the noisiness of the new rooms into which he had moved. On the latter subject he gives much detail, and these passages are the most arresting ones. He finds his life as an official more and more difficult; among his reproaches—and he does not spare Felice with these—the hardest one is leveled against her wish to live in Prague with him. Prague for him is unendurable, and to escape it he considers joining the army. The worst misery inflicted on him by the war, he writes, is his having no part in it; but it is not impossible that his turn will come: soon he will be drafted, Felice should wish that he will be accepted, as he would like to be. But nothing comes of it, in spite of repeated attempts, and he remains in his Prague office, "desperate, like a caged rat" (462).

She sends him Flaubert's *Salammbô*, with a very sad inscription. Reading it makes him unhappy, and for once he tries writing her a letter of comfort: "Nothing has ended, there is no darkness, no cold. ... Listen, Felice, the only thing that has happened is that my letters have become less frequent and different. What was the result of those more frequent and different letters? You know it. We must start afresh" (453).

Perhaps it is her *Salammbô* inscription that moves him to meet her and Grete Bloch in Bohemian Switzerland at Whitsun. For both of them it is the only bright moment of the year. The presence of Grete Bloch may have contributed to the success of these two days. Some of the rigid horror of the "tribunal" to which he had been subjected by the two women might have faded away at this meeting. Felice had a toothache, he was "allowed to fetch the aspirin" and to show his affection "face to face in the passage" (464). She should have seen him, he wrote just after his return to Prague, seeking among the lilacs "memories of [her] and her room" (455) throughout the long journey home. Normally he never took anything of the kind on a journey, since he did not like flowers. And the next day he writes that he is afraid he may have stayed there too long. Two days may have been too much. After a single day "it is easy to get away, but two days create ties which are painful to break" (455).

Not many weeks later, in June, yet another meeting took place in Karlsbad. This time it was short, and everything went very badly. Nothing more precise is known about it, but in a later letter there is mention of Karlsbad and of the "truly horrible journey to Aussig" (457). It must have been a particularly bad time, coming so soon after the good days at Whitsun, because Karlsbad hereafter figures on his list of the most painful moments, beside the Tiergarten and the Askanische Hof.

From now on he hardly writes anymore, or he rebuffs her complaints about his silence: "Why don't you write?"—he says to himself—"Why are you tormenting F.? That you are tormenting her is surely quite obvious, from her postcards. You promise to write, and don't. You send a telegram 'letter on way,' but there is no letter on the way; it doesn't get written until 2 days later. Once in a while and as an exception, a girl might be permitted to behave in this way" (456). The reversal is obvious: he is now doing to her precisely what she had done to him years before, and his mention of girls' being permitted to behave in this way does not exactly indicate that he was unaware of this reversal.

From August until December she hears nothing from him; and when later he does write, now and then, it is almost always to counter a suggestion of hers that they should meet. "It would be nice to meet; nevertheless we should not do so. Once again it would only be temporary, and we have suffered enough from temporary expedients" (459). "But all things considered, it's better that you don't come" (460). "As long as I am not free I don't wish to be seen, and I don't wish to see you" (463). "I warn you, as well as myself, against meeting; think seriously of earlier meetings and you will cease to want it. . . . So no meeting" (464).

The last passage quoted occurs in a letter dated as late as April 1916, and in context it sounds much more harsh. The Whitsun 1915 intermezzo excepted, the last eighteen months had seen a hardening of his defensive attitude, and one cannot anticipate any likelihood of change. But in the same month of April the name of Marienbad appears for the first time, on a postcard, and thereafter it recurs regularly. He is planning a vacation and would like to stay in Marienbad for three weeks, leading a quiet life there. The postcards now become more frequent. In mid-May he is actually in Marienbad on a business trip, and from there he at once writes to her a longish letter and a postcard:

"Marienbad is unbelievably beautiful. A long time ago I ought to have followed my instinct which tells me that the fattest are also the wisest. After all, one can diet anywhere, no need to pay homage to mineral springs, but only here can one wander about in woods such as these. Just now in fact the beauty is enhanced by the peace and solitude as well as by the eager receptivity of all things animate and inanimate; while it is hardly affected by the overcast and windy weather. I imagine if I were a Chinese and were about to go home (indeed I am a Chinese and am going home), I would make sure of returning soon, and at any price. How you would love it!" (468).

I have quoted this postcard almost in its entirety, because so many of Kafka's most essential proclivities and traits are gathered here in a very limited space: his love of the woods, his predilection for silence and emptiness, the question of thinness, and his almost superstitious respect for fat people. Silence and emptiness, the overcast, windy weather, receptivity of everything animate and inanimate—these are reminiscent of Taoism and of a Chinese landscape. And thus there is found here what is to my knowledge the only passage in which he says "Indeed I am a Chinese." The concluding statement, "How you would love it!" is his first real attempt for years to approach closer to Felice, and out of it came the happy Marienbad days.

The negotiations—one can hardly call them otherwise—for a vacation together last another month and animate the correspondence in a quite extraordinary way. Felice, thinking to please him, even suggests they go to a sanatorium. Perhaps she has a vague memory of the Riva sanatorium, where the company of "the Swiss girl" had been a blessing to him. But he does not like this suggestion; a sanatorium is "another office almost, in the service of the body" (471). He prefers a hotel. From July 3 to July 13, Kafka and Felice spend ten days together at Marienbad.

He left the Prague office in exemplary order, he was happy to be leaving it; if his departure had been forever he would have been "prepared to scrub every one of the stairs, on my knees, from attic to cellar, in order thus to demonstrate gratitude for being allowed to leave."[47] In Marienbad, Felice met him at the station. He spent the first night in an ugly room opening on a courtyard. But the next day he moved into an "extraordinarily beautiful room"[48] in the Hotel Balmoral. There he lived next door to Felice, each of them having a key to the communicating door. Headache and insomnia were bad; during the first days, and especially at night, he felt tormented and desperate. The entries in his diary tell how badly things were going. On July 8, he went with Felice on an excursion to Tepl, in miserable weather, but then the afternoon turned out to be "wonderfully light and beautiful,"[49] and that was the turning point. There followed five happy days with her; a single day, one feels like saying, for each of their five years. He wrote in his diary: "I have never yet been intimate with a woman apart from that time in Zuckmantel. And then again with the Swiss girl in Riva. The first was a woman, and I was ignorant; the second a child, and I was utterly confused. With F. I knew intimacy only in letters, in a human way not until the last two days. The clarity is still lacking, doubts remain. But it is beautiful, the gaze of her calm eyes, the opening of womanly depth."[50]

The evening before Felice left he started a long letter to Max Brod, which he finished only later, after she had gone: "But now I saw the look of trust in a woman's eyes and I could not shut myself off. . . . I have no right to resist it, even less so since I would myself voluntarily bring it about, if it were not to occur of itself, simply in order to receive that look again. I really didn't know her; aside from other doubts, I was impeded, earlier, precisely by fear of the reality of this letter-writing woman; when she came toward me across the big room, to receive the kiss of betrothal, a shudder went through me; the engagement expedition with my parents was, every stage of it, a torture for me; what terrified me most was being alone with F. before marriage. Now things have changed and are well. Our agreement is, briefly, to get married soon after the end of the war, to take two or three rooms in a Berlin suburb, each of us providing for his or her own domestic needs. F. will continue to work as heretofore, and I, well, I can't tell yet. . . . Nonetheless—the situation is calm, definite, and thus it has real possibilities. . . . After the morning in Tepl I experienced such lovely and winged days as I did not believe possible for me. Naturally some dark moments came between, but the beautiful and the light had the upper hand."[51]

On the last day of their vacation he took Felice to Franzensbad, where they visited his mother and one of his sisters. Returning in the evening to Marienbad, where he proposed to spend ten more days, he found that his hotel room, which had been exceptionally quiet, had been assigned to new guests, and he had to move into Felice's room, which was noisier. So the first postcards after her departure are filled again with complaints, about noise, headaches, and sleeping badly. But after five more days he has got used to her room, and, following his usual slow reaction, his postcards are pervaded with a tenderness and a happiness which touch the reader to the heart, if only because they are so rare. It must be considered as a stroke of good fortune that he stayed on, after Felice's departure, in the places known to both of them. He went on the same walks in the Marienbad woods, ate the prescribed meals, which he hoped would increase his weight, at the same eating places. When evening came, he would sit on her balcony, at the same table, and write to her by the light of the lamp that was familiar to them both.

Everything is written on postcards; every day he sends her one, on some days two. The first has the opening "My poor dearest," for he is still feeling unwell; whenever he calls Felice "poor," he means himself, he is the poor one. "I am writing with your pen, your ink, sleeping in your bed, sitting on your balcony—this would be all right, but through the single door I can hear the noise in the corridor and the noise of couples on either side" (473). Here the noise still drowns everything else—otherwise he would hardly have struck such an odd note, with his "this would be all right" as sequel to what precedes it. The card ends with the statement: "I am on my way to the Dianahof, to think about you while staring at my butter dish" (474).

In a later card he tells her that despite sleeplessness and headaches he is getting fat, and he sends her, in its entirety, "yesterday's menu." Here, with their times of the day indicated precisely alongside, are the meals that one would expect of him: milk, honey, butter, cherries, etc., but at noon comes—unbelievable!—"beef, spinach, potatoes" (476).

So he has indeed given up some of his resistance to her—the menu is an important item in this love affair. He is getting "fat," he also eats meat; since he otherwise eats all the things that he had approved of previously, the compromise between them consists in the quantity of these things and in the "beef." So, during the Marienbad days, they also came closer to one another and were reconciled via an agreement about food. The routine of life at the spa calms Kafka and takes away his fear of Felice. After she has left, he continues to eat the same dishes, in the same places, and he tells her so, as a kind of declaration of love.

But he pays homage to her also in a less intimate, more exalted way: "Imagine, we were not even aware of the most distinguished visitor to Marienbad, a man in whom so many place their trust: the Rabbi from Belz, no doubt at present the chief representative of Hasidism. He has been here 3 weeks. Last night for the first time I joined him and some 10 of his entourage on their evening walk. . . . And you, my most distinguished visitor to Marienbad, how are you? No news as yet, content myself with what the familiar walks tell me—today, for instance, the promenade of sulks and secrets" (475).

On one occasion, having not heard from her for two days, he writes: "One was so spoiled by being together, two steps to the left and there was news for the asking" (477). In another card of that day comes this: "Dearest—am I over-doing the writing again, as in former days? In justification: I am sitting on your balcony, on your side of the table, it's as though the 2 sides of the table were the 2 sides of a pair of scales; as though the balance established on our good evenings had been upset; and I, alone on one side of the scales, were going down. Going down, because you are far away. That's why I am writing. . . . The silence here at present is almost as complete as I desire: the nightlight glowing on the balcony table, all other balconies deserted owing to the cold, no sound except a steady murmur from Kaiserstrasse which doesn't disturb me" (477).

In this instant he was free from fear. He sat at her side of the table, as if he were she, but the scales went down, because she was far away and he was writing to her. It was almost the silence he desired, his table was the only one on which the nightlight was burning, and it was not indifference on which the light was feeding. All the other balconies were cold and empty. The steady murmur from Kaiserstrasse was not disturbing.

At a time when he really had not known Felice, he had said that in relationships with people his fundamental feeling was fear and indifference. That statement had now lost its force. When the freedom of the nightlight was granted to him, he felt love as well. "Someone must watch, it is said. Someone must be there."

Any life is laughable if one knows it well enough. It is something serious and terrible if one knows it even better. Back in Prague, Kafka set about an enterprise that can be regarded either way. The image he had had of Felice before Marienbad was unbearable to him, and he devoted himself to the Herculean task of changing it. For a long time now, since Bodenbach, he had been seeing her clearly, and he had unsparingly remonstrated with her about the traits he found painful. But he had done this only intermittently and without hope, because there was nothing he could do to change her. In Marienbad they talked about the Jewish People's Home in Berlin, where refugees and refugee children were cared for, and Felice had spontaneously uttered the wish to work there in her spare time. He had spoken of the place without expectation or purpose in mind, and he was delighted when she "tackled the idea of the Home quite independently and very well" (500). From now on, he had hopes for her; and, with that tenacity which in his case substituted for strength, he urged upon her in every letter to Berlin the practical realization of her plan to contact the Home. For three or four months, until the beginning of November, he wrote to her almost every day, and the People's Home was by far the most important topic of his letters, if not the only one.

Felice made hesitant inquiries about the Home; she was afraid that perhaps only students were allowed to work there. In his reply to this, he could not understand how she came to have this opinion: "Needless to say, it was students (of both sexes)—commonly the least selfish, most determined, most restless and exacting, keenest, most independent and farsighted of people—who started the venture and run it; but everyone alive has as much right to be part of it" (481). (It would be hard to find another passage in Kafka where there are so many superlatives.) To offer one's services to the Home would be "a hundred times more important" than the theater, or Klabund, or anything else (481). Besides, a high degree of self-interest would be involved. One would not be helping, but seeking help; from these exertions more honey could be gathered than from all the flowers in the woods of Marienbad; and he is positively voracious for news of her participation. As for Zionism, with which she was not sufficiently familiar, she should have no fears. Through the People's Home other aptitudes of hers would be realized, and he was much more interested in what these might lead to.

While still in Marienbad he had read a book about the life of Countess Zinzendorf; he admired her attitude to life and her "almost superhuman task" of directing the church of the Moravian Brethren in Herrnhut (517). He refers to her often, and in all his counsels at this time she occupies his mind as a model for Felice, an entirely unattainable one, to be sure. "On arriving after her wedding at her new flat in Dresden, which her Grandmother Zinzendorf had had furnished for the young couple in what was then considered an affluent manner, the Countess, aged 22, burst into tears" (484). Then follows a pious statement made by the young countess, about her being innocent of these frivolities, and asking for God's grace that He may keep her soul steadfast and avert her eyes from all the follies of this world. Kafka adds: "To be cut in stone and set in place above the furniture store."

In due course, what began as a desire to influence Felice becomes a regular campaign, and it is clear what the real issue is. He wants to rid her of bourgeois traits, so to speak, to move the furniture out of her, which, to his mind, embodies the most terrifying and odious aspect of bourgeois marriage. She is to learn how little significance should be attached to office work and family, as corollaries of selfishness; and he contrasts these with the humble activity of helping in a home for refugee children. But the parsonical overbearingness with which he harries her is something of which one would not have thought him capable. He asks for information about every step that brings her closer to the People's Home, and then about every detail of her activity there, once she has been accepted. There is one letter in which he puts twenty questions to her about her work; his voracity increases, and he becomes insatiable for news about it. He spurs her on, criticizes her, collaborates in the writing of a talk that she is to give at the Home, and he reads and studies for this purpose Friedrich Wilhelm Förster's *Jugendlehre*. He hunts for books for the children in the Home, even sends her from Prague several works edited for young people which he considers especially suitable, keeps referring to them in his letters with a meticulousness that is tantamount to pedantry, asks for photographs of Felice among her children, whom he wants to know by precise observation from a distance. He showers praises upon Felice when he is pleased with her, and this praise sounds so intense that she must have thought it a sign of love—and it comes whenever she follows his instructions. Gradually it does come to be a sort of subordination and obedience that he expects from her. The rectification of her image, the changing of her character, without which he cannot conceive of living with her in the future, turns into control of her.

Thus he shares in her activity, although he himself

lacks, as he says in one letter, the necessary dedication; she acts for him in what she is doing. He, contrariwise, needs more and more solitude; he finds it on Sunday walks in the environs of Prague, at first in company with his sister Ottla, whom he admires as if she were his betrothed. An acquaintance from his firm, who meets them on a walk, thinks that Ottla is his fiancée, and he shows no hesitation in telling Felice about this.

He now has a new kind of pleasure for his spare time: lying in the grass. "While lying there the other day, almost in the ditch (this year, however, the grass is tall and thick, even in the ditch), a rather distinguished gentleman, with whom occasionally I have official dealings, passed by in a carriage-and-pair on his way to an even more distinguished party. I stretched myself and experienced the joys . . . of being déclassé" (482). On a walk in the vicinity of Prague with Ottla, he discovers two wonderful places, both "as silent as the Garden of Eden after the expulsion of Man" (497). Later he goes for solitary walks: "Do you know the joys of being alone, walking alone, lying in the sun alone? . . . Have you ever walked a long way by yourself? The ability to enjoy it presupposes a great deal of past misery as well as past joys. As a boy I was alone a lot, but it was more from force of circumstance, rarely from choice. Now, however, I rush toward being alone as rivers rush toward the sea" (510). On another occasion he writes: "Walked a very long way, roughly 5 hours, alone yet not alone enough, in deserted valleys, yet not deserted enough" (523).

During this time he is preparing himself mentally for the life in the country which he was to share with Ottla in Zürau one year later; meanwhile, he attempts to tie Felice more and more strongly to the community of the Jewish People's Home in Berlin. During the week he lives his official's life, which fills him increasingly with disgust, so much so that he is still thinking of escaping from it by enlisting: as a soldier at least one would not be pampering oneself. Yet Felice is his vindication—because of her activities at the People's Home.

But he often mentions his writing, too, in his letters of this time. Since it is a period in which he feels incapable of any new work, he sends news about the fate of earlier stories, about publications and reviews. In September he announces that he has been invited to give a reading in Munich. He likes to read aloud and has a fancy to go; he would like her to be there: he rejects her suggestions about a meeting in Berlin or Prague. He is scared away from Berlin by his memory of events when they became engaged and of the "tribunal," which he seldom mentions in his letters, of course—two years have elapsed. But when a Berlin place-name brings the past to mind, he does not hesitate to let it be known how fresh the wounds of that time still are for him. What deters him from a meeting in Prague is his family: inevitably Felice would have to sit at his parents' table, and her involvement would strengthen the family's predominance, that superior power he continuously opposes with what strength he can muster. In keeping Felice away from Prague, he behaves like a politician trying to prevent an alliance between two potential enemies. Thus he sticks obstinately to his plan for a meeting in Munich. For two months they correspond on the subject. He knows that a reading would be a source of strength for him; Felice, too, now that she is concerned and obedient, gives him strength. In Munich, both sources are to be joined, each intensifying the other.

Yet this does not make his manner of reaching a decision any less peculiar. Once again one finds the familiar hithering and thithering: the journey is probable, but not yet certain, there are external threats that might spoil all the plans. After two months of discussion he writes, five days before the reading is due: "My journey is becoming more and more probable every day. In any case on Wednesday or Thursday I will send you a telegram with the lovely words: 'We are going' or the sad word: 'No' " (533). On the Friday, he goes.

The ineradicable peculiarity of Kafka's cast of mind is shown by his inability to learn from mistakes. Failure multiplied by failure does not, in his case, equal success. The difficulties always remain the same ones, as if to demonstrate that they are by nature insuperable. From countless considerations and calculations he systematically omits what might bring them to an auspicious conclusion. The freedom to fail is preserved, as a sort of supreme law, which guarantees escape at every fresh juncture. One is inclined to call this the freedom of the weak person who seeks salvation in defeat. His true uniqueness, his special relation to power, is expressed in the prohibition of victory. All calculations originate and end in impotence.

Thus, in spite of the experience gained from previous meetings, meetings that were wrong and short-lived, he was now staking his achievement of these four months—control over Felice by means of the Berlin People's Home —on the success of a single Saturday afternoon in Munich. Everything in Munich was unfamiliar to him: the places, the people, the procedure of the reading on Friday after a full day's train journey, and the sequel on Saturday. But he risked it, as if it enshrined a secret possibility of freedom. They had a quarrel in a "ghastly pastry shop" (534); no precise details are known about this. Felice, who had tried to oblige him for so long, seems to have rebelled. Probably her sudden outburst was not distinguished by subtlety. She reproached him with selfishness, and it was an old reproach. He could not simply accept it; it hurt him, for, as he himself later wrote, it was true. But his greatest selfishness, by far his greatest, was his self-will, and this only admitted reproaches that he leveled against himself: "My sense of guilt is strong enough at any time, it doesn't need feeding from outside; my constitution, on the other hand, is not strong enough to gulp down this kind of food very often" (534).

Thus the second flowering of their relationship came to an end. For four months this narrowest basis of understanding had held firm. One can indeed compare these four months with the first period, from September to December 1912; common to both was the hope and the strength that Kafka drew from Felice. But the first period was an ecstasy of writing, whereas during the second it was a question of working a change in Felice's character and adjusting her to his values. Disillusionment brought, after the first period, an end to his writing. After the second period the effect of estrangement was the reverse: it led him back to writing.

He returned from Munich with renewed spirits. The reading there was a "grandiose failure" (536); he had read "In the Penal Colony." "I had arrived, with my story as vehicle for the journey, in a town that meant nothing to me, except as a meeting place and a forlorn memory of youth, read there my filthy story with complete indifference, an empty stove-opening couldn't be colder, and was then, a rare occurrence for me in this place, together with people I didn't know."[52] The reviews were unfavorable, he agreed with them that it was incredibly impudent of him to read in public after not having written anything (so he said, exaggerating) for two years. (But in Munich he had also discovered that Rilke thought highly of his work, liking especially "The Stoker," which he preferred to *The Metamorphosis* and "In the Penal Colony.") Yet precisely this impudence—the public appearance, the fact that verdicts, mainly negative ones, had been pronounced, the defeat and the grandioseness of the failure amid unknown people—all this lent Kafka wings. If one also takes into account his quarrel with Felice, which enabled him inwardly to distance himself from her—the distance without which he could not write—then his renewed spirits on his return become understandable.

At once he set about finding an apartment, and this time he was lucky: Ottla arranged a room for him to write in, in a cottage on Alchemists' Lane which she had rented for herself. Here it was quiet enough, and he soon settled in. He declined to see Felice at Christmas, and for the first time in four years it is she who complains of a headache—she had taken over his. Almost disdainfully he mentioned the Home, so much discussed before. Now the Home must fulfill its function: to hold her interest and give her strength, but no more than that.

He had good moments in Ottla's house; things are better than at any time during the past two years. "A strange feeling, locking up one's house on a starlit night in this narrow street" (537). "It's wonderful living there, wonderful strolling home around midnight, down the old castle steps, into the city" (538). Here he wrote "A Country Doctor," "The New Advocate," "Up in the Gallery," "Jackals and Arabs," and "The Next Village," which were later included in the book *A Country Doctor*. Here he wrote "The Bridge," "The Hunter Gracchus," and "The Bucket Rider." Features common to all these stories were spaciousness, transformation (no longer into something small), and movement.

Not very much can be learned about the last phase of the relationship from Kafka's letters. The letter written at the turn of the year 1916–17, describing in detail and (as Kafka was to write in self-reproach) "calculatingly" the advantages and disadvantages of an apartment in the Schönborn Palace, with six points against and five points for it, carries the implication that they were planning to set up house together after the war. In this apartment, which would be ready made for her, Felice would be able to recuperate, for at least two or three months. She would, of course, have to do without a kitchen and a bathroom. It cannot be said that her presence is taken into account very convincingly; she figures only once during the enumeration of the eleven points for and against. Nonetheless, she does figure, and what is perhaps more important, she is asked to consider carefully and to give advice.

Not a single letter or postcard has been preserved from the first eight months of 1917; yet he must surely have written to her during that time. The first letter comes in September. In February Kafka had moved into an apartment in the Schönborn Palace. Here, more stories of the *Country Doctor* collection were written, as well as several texts that were not published during his lifetime, such as "The Great Wall of China." He is not altogether dissatisfied with this period, affirming as much in a letter of July 1917 to Kurt Wolff.

What occurred between Kafka and Felice in July 1917 can only be told from other sources; accordingly, it cannot be described as exactly as the foregoing. This July is the month of the second official engagement. The war was by no means over yet, and it seems that the original plan was brought forward somewhat. Felice came to Prague; sometimes it is supposed that she stayed at the Schönborn Palace, but there are reasons for doubting this. Kafka and she paid official engagement visits to friends of his. Max Brod noted the wooden and slightly ridiculous character of such a visit at his home. Once again, too, there was a search for furniture and an apartment. Perhaps Felice was not satisfied with the Schönborn Palace and insisted, to start with, on having a bathroom and a kitchen. She was carrying in her purse the unusually large sum of nine hundred kronen. In a letter to Frau Weltsch about the temporary loss of this purse, Kafka writes formally of his "fiancée." He may have overtaxed himself with official excursions and titles of this kind. Earlier it was said that it was not in his nature to learn from previous experiences. Or perhaps, without altogether knowing it, he was investing in pressures of the old kind, in order to *force* himself to escape. In the second half of July, he traveled with Felice to visit her sister at Arad in Hungary. During this journey there must have been a serious quarrel between them. Perhaps the confrontation with a member of her family was needed to induce a break. In Budapest he left Felice and returned to Prague via Vienna, alone. Rudolf Fuchs, whom Kafka saw in Vienna at that time, observes in his memoirs that Kafka spoke as if a definite break had occurred or was intended. Kafka wrote two letters to Felice from Prague, which have not survived; in these he probably made the situation quite plain to her.

He actually was determined to break with her now, but since he could not summon the strength to do so on his own, there ensued, two days after the second of these two Prague letters, during the night of August 9–10, 1917, his hemorrhage. A much later description gives one the impression that he exaggerated somewhat the duration of this hemorrhage. But there can be no doubt that suddenly late at night he lost a great deal of blood from his lungs, and that this explosive event—a poetic event, one might say, with its *imago* of a "bloody wound"—had very serious consequences for him. Although he felt relieved afterward, he consulted his doctor, the one whose physical bulk had such a calming effect (499), Dr. Mühlstein. How the latter reacted is not clear, but Kafka's account was sufficient to frighten Brod. Several weeks passed before Brod could persuade Kafka to consult a specialist. For Kafka had been from the start in no doubt as to the true grounds of his sickness; and not even the prospect of that freedom which was of paramount importance to him made it easy for him to surrender forever to the official medical science he had so stubbornly distrusted. His visit to the specialist on September 4 marked the beginning of a new period in his life. The pronouncement from this authoritative quarter, which he now compelled himself to recognize, freed him from Felice, from his fear of the marriage, and from the profession he hated. But it tied him forever to his sickness, of which he was to die, and which at this juncture was perhaps not very serious.

Indeed, the earliest statement about the specialist's findings, to be found in Brod's diary entry for the same date, does not sound so very serious. Catarrh at the extremity of one lung is mentioned, and a *danger* of tuberculosis. The fever, as it turned out, soon left Kafka altogether. But the unaccustomed medical procedures led to the crystallization of a plan of escape, absolutely necessary for Kafka's psychological survival. It was decided that he would have to go and live—provisionally for three months—in the country. The whereabouts for this had been prepared—one can hardly put it otherwise—long before: Ottla's farm in Zürau. Felice heard nothing of these matters for four weeks. Only on September 9, three days before he left for Zürau, when every stage of the move had been rigidly settled, did Kafka finally write her a first and very serious letter. Perhaps he might have openly informed her in this letter of his firm resolve to break with her forever. But she, after not replying to his two letters of August, had meanwhile written again in a conciliatory way, as if there were no serious obstacle between them, and he had received this friendly letter of hers, most inconveniently for him, on September 5, the day after his last consultation with the specialist. "Today," he writes to Brod, "letters came from F., calm, friendly, without any resentment, just as I see her in my fondest dreams. It is difficult now to write to her."[53]

But he does write on September 9, and he informs her, with dramatic brevity, of the events affecting his lungs. There is much talk of blood and emphatically of tuberculosis. In his own interest, he is not being given a pension but remaining as an official on active duty, and he is taking at least three months' vacation. Parents should not be told anything for the time being. The only note that she might in the long run have found threatening to herself is the conclusion. He writes: "Poor dear Felice," and this time the word "poor," so familiar from his correspondence, does sound—now that he is writing about his sickness—as if it refers for the first time not to him but to her. "It's not a knife that stabs only forward but one that wheels around and stabs back as well" (544).

In a postscript he adds that he has been feeling better since the hemorrhage. That was true; but perhaps, by saying this, he wanted to prevent her from coming in sudden alarm to visit him.

On September 12 the period in Zürau begins. The very first letter to Brod sounds like a message from a different world. On the first day he did not settle down to writing, because he found everything so delightful; also, he did not want to exaggerate, as he would have felt forced to do. But there is delight on the day after, as well: "Ottla really does carry me on her wings through the difficult world, the room ... is excellent, airy, warm, and all this in a house that's almost entirely quiet; everything I'm supposed to eat is round about me, plenteously, . . . and freedom, freedom above all. . . . In any case my attitude to tuberculosis today is like that of a child clinging to its mother's skirts. . . . Sometimes it seems that brain and lung had struck an agreement, without my knowledge. 'It can't go on like this,' said the brain, and after five years the lung announced that it was willing to help."[54]

And in his next letter he writes: "I live with Ottla in a wedlock that is small and good, not on the basis of the usual violently contained current, but of the small windings of a current flowing clear and straight. We have a nice household, in which both of you, I hope, will be happy."[55] Yet a shadow falls across this letter: "F. has announced that she is coming, a few lines. . . . I cannot understand her, she is extraordinary."[56]

She arrived; there is a reference to her visit in his diary: "September 21. F. was here, traveled thirty hours to see me; I should have prevented her. As I see it, she is suffering the utmost misery and the guilt is essentially mine. I myself am unable to take hold of myself, am as helpless as I am unfeeling, think of the disturbance of a few of my comforts and, as my only concession, condescend to act my part."[57]

The last letter but one to Felice, the longest, written ten days after her visit to Zürau, is the most disagreeable letter he ever wrote; it is a struggle to quote from it. She has written twice in the meantime. At first he does not open her letters but puts them aside. He tells her this at the very beginning, as well as the fact that he did read them later. What he finds in them puts him to shame, but he has for a long time been seeing himself more clearly than she has done, and he intends to explain what it is that he sees.

There follows the myth about the two combatants within him. It is an unworthy myth and a false one. The image of a struggle cannot encompass his inner processes; he distorts them by a kind of heroizing of his hemorrhage, as if the struggle were indeed a bloody one. But even if one were to allow that the image had some validity, it lures Kafka into stating another untruth: that he has come, during recent days, to doubt least of all that the better combatant, as he writes, belongs to her. Yet one knows that this struggle, or whatever one may call it, came to an end long ago, and that nothing belongs to her anymore, and least of all during these last days. Should it be thought that he intended this untruthful assertion to be a solace for her, something like a gallant courtesy extended to the woman humiliated and rejected? Be that as it may, not much later there comes a statement that can justly be cited as being authentic Kafka: "I am a mendacious creature; for me it is the only way to maintain an even keel, my boat is fragile" (545). This forms the transition to a longish paragraph which summarizes his insights into himself. It is well written, it belongs to literature; Kafka liked it so well that he transcribed it verbatim into a letter to Max Brod, and again into his diary. That is where it belongs, and readers will realize why it is not included in the present account. Then comes another fairly long section about the changing fate of both combatants and the flow of blood. It leads into a matter that is of serious concern to him: "I don't believe this illness to be tuberculosis, at least not primarily tuberculosis, but rather a sign of my general bankruptcy" (545). Yet the blood and the combat are not yet done with, and further inferences are drawn from them. Suddenly light dawns, in this passage: "Please don't ask why I put up a barrier. Don't humiliate me in this way" (545). Here he starkly says that he is putting her from him, and that there is no explanation for it—and if the letter consisted of just these two sentences, it would have the force of a biblical utterance. However, he weakens it immediately by making an empty gesture, yet all at once the truth comes out: "My actual, or rather, . . . my alleged tuberculosis," he says, "is a weapon compared to which the countless others used earlier, ranging from 'physical incapacity' up to my 'work' and down to my 'parsimony,' look expedient and primitive" (545–46).

Finally he tells her a secret, in which even he does not believe at present, but which must be true: he will never be well again. With this he kills himself off for her, and he withdraws from her now by a kind of suicide projected into the future.

Thus, most of this letter was dictated by an endeavor to evade further impositions from her side. Since he had not the slightest feeling left for her, he had no real solace to give her. From his Zürau happiness, which was a happiness of freedom, he could not extract any show of sorrow or even of regret.

The last letter to Felice is dated October 16, and it reads as if it were hardly written for her. He puts her far from him, although she is already far away; his glassy statements do not include her and are addressed as to a third person. He begins with a quotation from a letter from Max Brod: Brod had written that Kafka's letters bore witness to a great tranquility, as if he were happy in his misfortune. As confirmation of this, Kafka now gives a description of Felice's last visit. Perhaps it is accurate; certainly it is cold as ice: "You were unhappy about the pointlessness of your journey, about my incomprehensible behavior, about everything. I was not unhappy" (546). He felt his misery less, once he had seen and acknowledged it, and remained calm in this knowledge, his lips shut tight, very tight. The greater part of the letter consists of a reply written to Max Brod, approximately quoted, and mailed four days previously. He then tells her that his physical condition is excellent; he hardly ventures to ask about hers. He says that he has given Max, Felix Weltsch, and Oskar Baum detailed reasons why they should not visit him—a warning to her not to come again.

The last paragraph runs: "I don't know Kant, but the sentence is surely applicable to nations only; it would hardly apply to civil wars, to 'inner wars,' where peace would be of a kind desirable only for one's ashes" (547).

With this he rebuffs the wish for a reconciliation which Felice had disguised in a quotation from Kant. With the peace that one desires for one's ashes, he withdrew behind death even more emphatically than at the end of the previous letter. There is not a word about ashes in any of his detailed correspondence with friends at this time.

There is no justification in the fact that the sickness, which had begun as a means to an end, eventually did become real. The true justification appears in that new series of observations—the "Third Octavo Notebook"—which he began to write two days after his last letter to Felice. The diary he had earlier kept breaks off for more than a year. The penultimate entry for 1917—coming late in the day, one might say—contains the following statement: "I haven't yet written down the decisive thing, I am still going in two directions. The work awaiting me is enormous."[58]

NOTES

1. Franz Kafka, *Briefe: 1902-1924* (New York: Schocken Books; Frankfurt am Main: S. Fischer Verlag, 1958), p. 102.

2. Franz Kafka, *Diaries*. Vol. I: 1910-1913; Vol. II: 1914-1923 (New York: Schocken Books, 1948, 1949; London: Martin Secker & Warburg, 1949); hereafter cited as *Diaries*, I, and *Diaries*, II. *Diaries*, I, p. 267.

3. *Ibid.*, pp. 268-69.

4. Probably so named after the muse of comedy, since the trip was largely devoted to visiting cultural sights.

5. *Briefe*, p. 97.

6. *Diaries*, I, p. 160.

7. *Ibid.*, p. 211. The "atrophied" phrase in the original reads literally: "I thinned down in all these directions."

8. *Briefe*, p. 98.

9. Franz Kafka, *Letter to His Father* (New York: Schocken Books, 1966), p. 19. Included in Franz Kafka, *Wedding Preparations in the Country* (London: Martin Secker & Warburg, 1954), p. 163.

10. A young Czech writer with whom Kafka formed an intimate friendship in 1920. See Franz Kafka, *Letters to Milena* (New York: Schocken Books; London: Martin Secker & Warburg, 1953).

11. *Letters to Milena*, p. 35.

12. Kafka mentions the encounter with the Swiss girl several times in his diaries (October 15, 20, and 22, 1913) and once in a letter to Max Brod, September 28, 1913 (*Diaries*, I, pp. 301, 303 ff.; II, p. 220; *Briefe*, p. 121). Kafka promised never to mention her name (*Diaries*, I, p. 304), and referred to her only by initials (G. or G.W.).

13. *Diaries*, II, p. 42.

14. Franz Kafka, *The Trial* (New York: Schocken Books, 1969), p. 19; (London: Martin Secker & Warburg, 1956), p. 27. (Hereafter page references are given for the American and British editions respectively.)

15. *Ibid.*, p. 21; p. 29.

16. *Ibid.*, p. 29; p. 38.

17. *Ibid.*, p. 30; p. 39.

18. *Diaries*, II, pp. 65–66.

19. *Ibid.*, p. 66.

20. *Ibid.*, pp. 68–69.

21. *The Trial*, p. 228; pp. 254–55.

22. *Ibid.*, p. 263; p. 290.

23. *Ibid.*, p. 225; p. 251.

24. *Ibid.*

25. *Ibid.*, p. 229; p. 255.

26. *Diaries*, II, p. 93.

27. *Ibid.*

28. *Ibid.*, p. 94.

29. *Ibid.*

30. *Ibid.*, p. 95.

31. *Ibid.*

31. *Ibid.*, p. 96.

33. *Ibid.*, pp. 98–99.

34. *Ibid.*, p. 100.

35. *Ibid.*, p. 106.

36. *Ibid.*, p. 108.

37. *Ibid.*, p. 111.

38. *Ibid.*, pp. 111–13.

39. Franz Kafka, *The Penal Colony* (New York: Schocken Books, 1948), p. 191; *In the Penal Settlement* (London: Martin Secker & Warburg, 1949), p. 185.

40. *Krachmandel* are soft-shelled almonds; however, idiomatically *Krach* means "quarrel."

41. Franz Kafka, *Dearest Father* (New York: Schocken Books, 1954), p. 295; *Wedding Preparations in the Country* (London: Martin Secker & Warburg, 1954), p. 324.

42. *Ibid.*, pp. 294–95; p. 323.

43. *The Penal Colony*, p. 147; *In the Penal Settlement*, p. 143.

44. *Briefe*, p. 29.

45. *Diaries*, II, p. 87.

46. *Dearest Father*, p. 45; *Wedding Preparations in the Country*, p. 49.

47. *Briefe*, p. 137.

48. *Ibid.*

49. *Ibid.*, p. 138.

50. *Diaries*, II, p. 159. The passage from "With F. I knew . . ." to the end does not appear in the German *Tagebücher* or in the English *Diaries*. The source is the manuscript of the diaries as cited by Klaus Wagenbach in his *Franz Kafka in Selbstzeugnissen und Bilddokumenten* (Hamburg: Ernst Rowohlt Verlag, 1964), p. 101.

51. *Briefe*, pp. 139–40.

52. *Ibid.*, p. 153.

53. *Ibid.*, p. 160.

54. *Ibid.*, p. 161.

55. *Ibid.*, p. 165.

56. *Ibid.*, p. 164.

57. *Diaries*, II, pp. 184–85.

58. *Ibid.*, p. 190.